Merging with the
Beloved

Merging with the **Beloved**

Mystical Path to Oneness

Vinita Dubey

PARTRIDGE

Print information available on the last page.

To order additional copies of this book, contact
Partridge India
000 800 10062 62
orders.india@partridgepublishing.com

www.partridgepublishing.com/india

Contents

Om Swastih[1]
Om Namo Narayanayah!

Inspired by Lord Vēṅkaṭēśvarā
For the love of Giridhārī.
With immense gratitude for Meena Om.

---

[1] *Om* – sound vibration for cosmic consciousness. *Swastih* – auspiciousness, prosperity, blessings

Acknowledgements

I would like to offer my eternal love and gratitude to my mother who is the only one who loves me so unconditionally. To my two sons with whom I share my deepest love, who have made my life worth living, I want to offer this book as a gift of devotion. May it blossom in their hearts.

My deepest respects for my Guru, Sri Sri Ravi Shankar. I have learnt so much from him. I have made spiritual connections with so many in the Art of Living family. We share our journey and it's beautiful.

I am most grateful to Meenaji for her loving support and exemplary devotion. She is a mirror of my soul, a divine mother, an Avatar, a presence of Krisn consciousness. My love and gratitude to all the Pranam Bandhu co-travelers, like Anjali, who have been there with me through this journey - we have been a support for each other.

I want to recognize the role Sal Rachele has had in my life in the last few years. I am truly thankful for his enlightened guidance, mentoring, support, healing and loving service towards my evolution. I am deeply grateful to all the masters who have been there to serve me with their unconditional love and support.

My sincere respects to Nanaji who has always been there selflessly to guide me for my growth. Without him my trip to Vrindavan would have been quite empty.

My whole family has been so supporting and loving. A special thanks to Madhu who's like family to me. All the friends with whom I'm connected on heart and soul level have been an integral part of my journey. A sincere friend is truly a blessing. There are online spiritual communities now, and SpeakingTree is one such where I've made close friends and we support each other in our journey towards enlightenment.

We are here for each other. We are all connected, we are all one, we are in this together. What is life without people? I am grateful for all the beautiful souls in my life.

Foreword by Sal Rachele

This is a book about love, devotion and spirituality. Coming from a scientific, mental background, it is, perhaps at first sight, curious that I am writing this Foreword. Just as the author originally set out on a different course and later found herself writing instead about devotion, so it is that many a soul begins the spiritual path with the "lure" of perhaps seeking a better life, escaping a deep pain or hurt, or following the promise of greater material riches.

The first thing one must do in order to cultivate a life of love, devotion and spirituality, is to focus on love. What is love? That might be one of the most often asked questions, maybe third only to "Who am I?" and "What is the meaning of life?"

Like so many things in life, we can see the effects of love, but not necessarily love itself. In looking at the lives of the saints, avatars, rishis, gurus and such, that are abundantly found within India and other countries, it is obvious to the careful observer that there is great love and devotion being radiated from their own beings. Their love is not just toward a given teacher or guide, but exists as a lifestyle among these beings.

What is it that captivates and hearts and minds of these great souls? What are they able to see that the average human being on Earth is unable to comprehend? Are they able to have a direct experience of *darshan* with a great master, even if that being has been out of body for a long time?

Possibly a deeper and more subtle question is, "What is the difference between idol worship and true reverence and devotion to a master or saint?"

In my own experience, idol worship implies a separation between self and the object or being that is worshiped. Somehow, we expect that being or object to magically take away our pain, or grant our wishes, or somehow do our spiritual work for us. True devotion, on the other hand, involves the recognition that some beings have gone before us and are capable of showing us the way. This is analogous to driving a well-traveled highway to get to our destination (except that many a spiritual path is a bit less traveled. The majority of souls on Earth choose a comfortable, familiar path.)

In other words, why re-invent the wheel when it comes to spiritual development? Why not study the lives of the masters and saints to see how they arrived at their various states of higher consciousness.

Another aspect of love, devotion and spirituality involves the humbling realization that most of us have only a tiny glimpse of true reverence and Divine Love.

I once remarked, in one of my workshops, that if we had even the tiniest understanding of how much love God has for each and every one of us, we would never have another problem in life, ever. All of our problems arise from the belief in separation from God, even though such separation may be presented in a myriad of forms. We make the mistake of believing in an angry, judgmental God that somehow demands sacrifice and obedience to a set of principles or commandments.

Part of being on the spiritual path is examining your own beliefs and attitudes and throwing out the ones that no longer serve you. We hope this book helps you embrace more fulfilling and rewarding ways of looking at life.

In this book, the author begins with a necessary amount of background information, utilizing mental processes and description of events, both in her own life and the lives of the many revered figures of Indian history. She then goes on to relate some of her more personal experiences of love and devotion. As the book progresses, the reader is taken into a more non-linear space, one that can barely be described in words at all.

If you are expecting a "How to" book, with charts, diagrams and step-by-step process on how to attain enlightenment and Divine Love, you might be disappointed. Instead, the author leads us into a deep heart space of appreciation for the many saints, gurus and masters she has encountered along her journey. I found myself in the temples of Krishna and others, right there with her, as I read her love-filled accounts of being in those places.

As you read this book, I urge you to get out of your head and into the transcendental aspects of heart. Allow the experience to be transferred directly into your soul.

Yours on the spiritual path.

--Sal Rachele
www.salrachele.com

Introduction

Journey Back to Devotion

Last summer we went to the Shiva-Vishnu temple in Livermore, CA. Someone in my family is a devotee of Balaji and he wanted to go to pay homage on the successful completion of some work.

It was pure coincidence that as soon as we entered the shrine the Archana (prayer service) started. We felt so blessed. Like we do, I was praying for my sons, mother, for other things, and then in a clear distinct masculine voice within, I heard, "And what about your book?"

I had written a book on Santana Dharma titled, "Eternal Way to Bliss". "My book?!" I was more surprised by the question than by the telepathic voice. I guess my sincere efforts at writing on Truth and *Dharma* were well recognized! Then I heard Him say something to the effect, "Write your next book on devotion. ON ME!" ending with a thunderous voice, immediately followed by the priest shouting, "Govinda! Govinda! Govinda!" It was uncanny. Then the priest proclaimed, "Balaji is Govinda". My Govind? I didn't even know that because I never had an inclination towards Venkatesh Balaji. My devotion has always naturally flowed towards Giridhari, i.e., Krishn.[2]

After that powerful experience, I stepped out of the shrine, wondering if it was my imagination. Still pondering as we left the temple I thought, "On devotion? What a lame subject!" I was keen on writing the second book on the practical applications of spirituality. Writing it like an Upanishad, a question and answer exchange between student and Guru. What transpired over the days and months that followed brought great clarity on why I should write on devotion. Situations and events just happened, and things started falling into place.

---

[2]   Although "Krishna" is the Western spelling of this Hindu Avatar, the authentic pronunciation is without the long 'a' sound at the end. It is कृष्ण in Devanagari script. The name "Krishna" with the 'a' sound at the end is feminine, e.g. the River Krishna.

Vinita Dubey

It is as per His calling that I embark on this journey. My expressions in this book are an offering to Govinda, to that eternal consciousness (*Chetana*) in all names and forms.

I wanted to start this book on the auspicious day of Dussehra, after the nine nights of Navratri; it is the tenth day of victory. It so happened that I planned a trip to India to be with my mother during this time. Then I decided to visit the hometown of Krishn, Mathura-Vrindavan for Dussera and start this book on devotion there. But then certain obstacles prevented me from being there during Dussera. Somehow things arranged themselves for me to be there on 29ᵗʰ October 2012, which I later realized was Sharad Purnima. Sharad Purnima was the full moon night of the full blossoming of divine love; the night of Krishn's divine dance, Raas, with the Gopis of Vrindavan. I could not believe I would be there on the spot where this happened on that very night! What a divine gift. What could be more auspicious and meaningful than to starting this book on the divine night of devotion.

On 23 Decemeber, 2012, it was Vaikunth Ekadasi, Gita Jayanti, in California, and again we went to the Balaji temple in Livermore. Of course I was waiting for a message, what do you think! I was in the shrine of my beloved Balaji waiting...in deep reverence and love. I heard a voice in my inner ear, just one sentence: "Vaikunth is your heart." My thought continued as, "And today the doors of your heart are open." Vaikunth is your heart? I pondered over this for several weeks. The Anahata chakra is the door to Vaikunth. So I guess it is through the heart that you reach Vaikunth. The heart is the inner self, not the physical heart. Later a Reiki master told me during a session that it's the only Chakra that radiates both outward towards the manifested ego and world, as well as inward towards the soul.

Aho! That's it! The pieces of the puzzle fit together now. Vaikunth, the abode of Narayana encompasses all the worlds of existence. Narayana epitomizes perfection in both the internal and external worlds. Narayana's Avatar Krishn exemplified this. Sri Krishn born on Ashtami the 8ᵗʰ day in the middle signifies this perfect balance. That's what I've come to attain in this life, not leave the mundane world and only be turned inward, but to move from individual consciousness to universal consciousness. I am going to learn from Krishn - the full blossoming of human potential.

"Janmashtami celebrates the birth of Lord Krishn. Ashtami is significant as it indicates a perfect balance between the seen and the unseen aspects of reality; the visible material world and the invisible spiritual realm.

His birth on Ashtami signifies His mastery of both spiritual and material worlds. He is a great teacher and spiritual inspiration as well as the consummate politician. On the one hand, he is Yogeshwara, the Lord of Yogas, while on the other, he is a mischievous thief.

The unique quality of Krishn is that he is at once more pious than the saints and yet a thorough mischief-monger! His behavior is a perfect balance of the extremes — perhaps this is why the personality of Krishn is so difficult to fathom. The Avdhoot is oblivious to the world outside, and a materialistic person, a politician or a king is oblivious to the spiritual world. But Krishn is both Dwarkadheesh and Yogeshwar.

Krishn's teachings are most relevant to our times in the sense that they neither let you get lost in material pursuits nor make you completely withdrawn. They rekindle your life, from being a burnt-out and stressed personality to a more centered and dynamic one. Krishn teaches us devotion with skill. To celebrate Gokulashtami is to imbibe extremely opposite yet compatible qualities and manifest them in your own life.

Know that you have to play a dual role — of being a responsible human being on the planet and at the same time to realize that you are above all events, the untouched Brahman. Imbibing a bit of *Avadhoot* and a bit of activism in your life is the real significance of celebrating Janamashtami.

"Krishn's life has all the nine Rasas or flavors. For instance, he was naughty like a child, a warrior, joy personified and a source of knowledge. He was a perfect friend and guru. Krishn was Poorna Kala Avatar, all the skills were present in Him." --Sri Sri Ravi Shankar

Now that the connection of my life with Narayana was clear, I still did not know what to write on devotion. For me, it's an experience that's very hard to express on paper. Most of the time my devotion is expressed when I sing bhajans (songs for the divine) and feel that intoxication, the ecstasy. How could I express my devotion in words? I started with my trip to

Mathura-Vrindavan and then halted again not knowing how to structure this book and with what content, what theme, what flow. I started listening to the Srimad Bhagavatam, the magnum opus on devotion. Swamiji said that the stories and praise of the Lord in this text are meant to cultivate and foster devotion in our hearts. I thought I should write about the glories of my Krishn. However; that too didn't seem to flow. It was then that I looked into my heart and saw what came. I should write about my story, my love for Krishn and His stories and His greatness would automatically be weaved in.

The first chapter of my books starts off gloomy; it states the problem, which is then responded to in the rest of the book. This is similar to how the Bhagavat Gita and Upanishads start. With misery or a question.

I decided to write about both unconditional love for others and devotion to the divine. Because one is incomplete without the other.

1

Stuti – Praise the Lord

सच्चिदानंद रूपाय विश्वोत्पत्यादि हेतवे
तापत्रय विनाशाय श्री कृष्णाय वयं नमः

Sachidanand rupaya vishvotpatyadi hetave
tapatraya vinashaya shri krishnaya vayam namah

L ike a ray of the sun, I have emerged from the One cosmic consciousness.

As though cell division, souls are created from source, and a family tree is created. Like a baby cell, I have descended from the cosmic Krishn[3] consciousness. Wandering through space and time, this soul has forgotten its connection, this cell feels separate from the body of consciousness.

This, what you are about to read, is a call from the source, to remember my oneness with it. By invoking His presence, by igniting my devotion, it is a trick by Krishn to bring me back to Him, to merge back into my Beloved.

God is personal, intimate as well as formless and transcendental. Multiplicity and oneness co-exist. The transcendental ultimate reality is like the canvas and a painting on it is the apparent reality. Like sound is a superimposition on silence, so is creation on consciousness. Consciousness is both immediate and transcendental.

Both happily co-exist; Krishn, my beloved Lord, and the one eternal universal consciousness (that I am). That one universal consciousness created this universe and also created several divine forms that the Hindus call by different names. These divine forms, Devis, Devatas, Avatars, were created to express different virtues and elements that govern this creation. One of them is Krishn; He is an avatar of Narayana, and the purpose of an avatar is to re-establish truth and goodness in every age. That universal consciousness created avatars for a reason and purpose, and avatars are the most transparent form of that consciousness on earth. Krishn Himself is consciousness, and my soul. He is both the means to the end and the end itself. True knowers of Krishn are those who have dropped the "I".

For me no one else exists except for Govind; this world is immaterial. Krishn is the only one who is always there for me, who will never change, and who loves me unconditionally, accepts me just as I am. He is my only support when I am down; He is my beloved when I'm in ecstasy. He is a friend I play with and cherish; He is like a father in whose lap I can lay.

---

[3] Although "Krishna" is the Western spelling of this Hindu Avatar, the authentic pronunciation is without the long 'a' sound at the end. It is कृष्ण in Devanagari script. The name "Krishna" with the 'a' sound at the end is feminine, e.g. the River Krishna.

Not only is Krishn my beloved but he is also my Guru. He delivers the highest knowledge for Moksha in the Bhagavat Gita. Krishn is consciousness and also the entire creation. First, Krishn talks about His universal Self in the Gita (chapters ten and eleven) before He talks about devotion in the twelfth chapter. Krishn, the epitome of devotion, talks about devotion! He is the most complete avatar. From being the cutest son, a playful and powerful cowherd boy, to the perfect lover, a noble king, a skilled politician, a great friend, the highest Guru, and every role he played with skill and perfection. His life exemplified the Gita itself in terms of devotion, knowledge, discipline, and skill in action. Sri Krishn held a flute in one hand and Sudarshan Chakra in the other. Meaning, he brought divine love without any lust, and also destroyed the evil elements prevalent at the time.

Sri Krishn has exemplified how one can be a King in the outer world, as Dwarka Dheesh (King of Dwarka), implementing spirituality in action; and king of the inner world, as Yogeshvar nath, giving the wisdom of the Gita. Being content spiritually is good but we have also come to bring change in the world.

He gave so many lessons on how to achieve this balance and perfection. One such is when Sri Krishn tells Draupadi and the Pandavs to forgive the Kauravs and go to war. You may ask, how can you go to war after forgiving? Forgiveness is inner wisdom that leads to outer action of war to protect righteousness and truth. War being the last resort when all else fails. As my friend Savitha, a Mahabharat expert, clarified that Krishnji told Draupadi that they "should do it [war] out of establishing righteousness and not revengeful attitude." Another way to look at it is, say a thief steals from you or someone murders your family member - you should forgive, and also take action for justice and righteousness; not just sit and do nothing. The court room is like Kurukshetra, and a constitution is like a scripture with laws according to common values.

Krishn is so smart, charming, skillful, extremely attractive and intelligent. He is my beloved, my Guru and my God. I know He's both personal and eternal. Knowledge supports devotion, devotion enchants knowledge.

Interestingly all the devotional saints of India in the fifteenth and sixteenth century experienced intense longing. That was the age of longing; this is the age of celebration. In the sense that when you have the knowledge, you know He is always with you, He is your soul, and He and you are one. Then there is celebration.

He is my soul; a projection of my soul is His *darshan* and then He disappears back into the eternity of my soul.

> *Within moments of an intention to invoke Him, He comes, filling me with His fragrance. Like fluid fills a bottle, He fills my frame as bliss. Two within one, like mind and soul, the separation fades, not knowing when it is Him when it is I.*

I am drunk with the cocktail of knowledge and devotion; there is no higher ecstasy than the intoxication of this nectar. It's the purest experience of human existence.

Truly devotion is the most beautiful.

Sing your Beloved's Name!
With the longing in your heart...call Him.
Hey Krishn Gopal Hare, Jai Nand Ke Laal Hare!
With the innocence of a child call Him.
Govinda Madhava...Gopala Keshava...Giridhari! Giridhari!
His sweet Presence comes and fills the air.
His Loving Light fills my being,
Till I do not know the boundaries of me or Him,
Intoxicated with His blissful presence,
Dissolved in an ecstasy beyond time...
Where everything swirls into nothingness.
He loves me so dearly. His tender sweet eyes, His faint smile.
Life is worth living when you are filled with the Divine...

Meera Bai's bhajans were her conversations with Krishn; in devotion words flow as poetry. It's very difficult to express devotion on paper, with words. Devotion is sung and has to be felt in person!

Meera Bai's bhajan:

"Pyare darshan dijo aaj, tum bina rahyo na jaye, darshan dijo aaj.
Jala bina kamala, chandra bin rajani, aise tum dekhya bin sajani.
Aakul vyakul firoon raina dina, viraha kaleja khaye, darshan dijo aaj.
Divasa na bhookh, neend nahi naina, mukh se kahata na aave baina.
Kyon tarasaao antarayaami, aana milo kirpa kar Swami.
Meera daasi janam-janam ki, padon tumhaari paaon, darshan dijo aaj."

Translation:
O beloved! Please come to me today, I can't be without you, please come to me today.
Like a pond without a lotus, a night without the moon, is my existence without seeing you.
Distressed and distraught I move day and night, this intense longing from separation is eating up my heart.
There's no hunger in the body, no sleep in the eyes, and unable to utter any words.

Why do you create this longing my divine indweller? Come to me,
   I plead to you O Lord!

"When you know you are God, how can you have this devotion and
fascination for Krishn, Mama?" my son asks me in astonishment. "On the
one hand, you say I am God, you are God, everyone is God...ok Brahman,
and then, on the other hand, you say pray to an eternal God - Krishn?!" He's
quite confused by my talk on Advaita and Bhakti at the same time.

"Knowing that Krishn and I are one, that there is only One, we can still play
the game of duality, and enjoy the bliss and ecstasy of devotion; and do so
knowingly", said I.

> *Aa apne rang se bhar do Murari*
> *Ek Rang Ban kar Mein Naachoongi*
> *Is Raas ki Raat Tujh Sang Bitaoongi*
> *Kesari ke Krishn...Krishn Mein Kesari*
> *Rass mein doobh kar mit gayi Kesari*

Translation:

> Fill me with Your presence Murari
> Merged in you I will dance in the bliss of ecstasy
> This dance of Maya on the eternal Void
> He is in me as me, I am in Him as Him....
> This great expanse flooded with bliss

> *I drink a spirit that doesn't come in a bottle, not a vintage, it's*
>   *eternal...*
> *Men drink spirits and lose sensibility, my senses are lost in thee*
>   *Manhari!*
> *I'm served the poison of negativity, turn to the nectar of love oh*
>   *Giridhari!*
> *Emotions I turn and sing to thee, the best remedy, now your people*
>   *call me deewani!*
> *I've found the solution to misery, it's the dance of Bhakti, now your*
>   *world calls me baawari!*

Piya me to baanwari ho gayi!
Akshaya prem se juddh gayi.
Magna nashe mein kho gayi!
Purna Anandit ho gayi.
Piya me to teri ho gayi...

When love becomes an offering to the divine – it's devotion
When eyes well up with tears of gratitude - know it's devotion
When love spreads its fragrance to all and all of creation – it's devotion
When love becomes a gentle breeze of grace – it's devotion
When love seeps into you unknowingly - know it's devotion
When you have nothing left to offer but your Being – it's devotion....
When love becomes a prayer – it's devotion
When love songs become bhajans – it's devotion
When conversations become a poem – it's devotion
When love knows not why it loves – it's devotion
When intoxication means ecstasy – it's devotion
When the mind twirls and the heart dances
like a Sufi – know that it's devotion

When love becomes sacred it's devotion
When the mind drops into prayer it's devotion
O Sweet devotion! I dance in your bliss!
When intoxicated singing His name it's devotion
When I sense my beloved as vast love everywhere, as
everything ...everyone, as all existence...it's supreme devotion
When I become that nectar of devotion, when the beloved
fills me...and merges...there's only devotion

The divine is present all the time, when I become aware, that instant
there's Darshan.

Krishn is always my soul but when the "I" drops, that moment
there's Darshan.

When I say I am Him and He is me the world thinks I'm crazy.

They praise my devotion of duality and can't relate to love as unity.

I AM Krishn..this child's play...this dance of duality...a *raas* in the
oneness of eternity.

7

Who is Krishn but consciousness; where is consciousness but all
that is!

Jai Krishn Gopal Hari... Hey deen dayal hare
Shyam ke rang me rang gayi Meera...Rass khan to rass ke khan hue

These are my conversations with Krishn:

For so long I have been calling Your name. Oh! This intense yearning!
So long I have been waiting. Oh! This intense longing! My mind and soul
immersed. Hey Giridhari! Come to me. Govind! Govind!! Govind!!! …

Ah, Giridhari! Finally, You have come! O Ghanshyam! You heard the call
of my soul and longing of my heart. So subtly You appear in this moonlit
night here in this forest. I am elated and transformed.

Oh, Govind! Your countenance, Your soft charming radiant face is
irresistible! Your faint naughty smile, and the twinkle in your eyes is so
captivating that my eyes can't move.

There could be no greater attraction in this world than Your presence, Your serene divine mesmerizing presence. In this night, Your twilight face shines like a thousand moons. This moment seems still and eternal while the whole world moves.

The gentle breeze through the trees, the scent of the night jasmine float through and yet we remain untouched, unmoved as if in eternal union.

May I forever rest in Your arms, surrender and feel that deep relief in my soul, then fall asleep while You play Your soothing flute. Oh! That is what my heart is longing for. But I can't move, I remain frozen looking at You, thoughtless, bodiless, and only soul.

A gush of wind flutters the peacock feather on Your crown, a lock of Your dark wavy hair brushes Your face. I look at You like a little girl whose jaw drops and head tilts. Then You smile at me with fondness and sweet love.

So overwhelmed am I with Your charm, magnanimity, and Your breathtaking divine presence that I feel I will swoon. I hear the divine musicians start to play: Veena, Tabla, Manjeera, and Sarod. Giridhari joins in with His flute. Oh! The sound...So soft and sweet! My mind merges and I am gone. All the Gods have come too, as no one even in heaven would want to miss this divine *darshan*.

You are looking so radiant, Giridhari, your glowing twilight blue color, and striking white mesmerizing eyes. The *Chandan* and *Kesar tilak* on Your forehead, the pearl earrings and flower necklaces. There is a scent of sandalwood in the air. I witness Your presence, Your shining orange silk upper cloth, dazzling yellow dhoti, and armlets of precious stones, Your tender graceful hands holding Your flute. I want to bow down and touch Your soft and gentle feet, a most heart-melting sight! Even the Gods are awed by Your brilliance.

As I witness the Lord, a *Stuti*[4] is being revealed. A beautiful melody and poetry start flowing from within.

　　"Sri Krishn Govind Hare Murare,

---

[4]　Stuti – Hymns in praise for the Lord

I bow down and surrender myself at Your feet.
In all the worlds besides You there is nothing so sweet...Hey Nath
Narayana Vasudeva.

Sri Krishn Govind Hare Murare,
Luckiest are those who can experience Your transcendental
presence.
Most compassionate is the Lord who showers His grace and
radiance...Hey Nath Narayana Vasudeva.

Sri Krishn Govind Hare Murare,
What words can this mind offer to one who is beyond expression.
I can sing for eons in Your praise yet it remains pale...Hey Nath
Narayana Vasudeva.

Sri Krishn Govind Hare Murare,
Beyond understanding are You yet my being is captivated by Your
love.
Oh Lord tell me what is the secret to that unknowable pull of Your
soul...Hey Nath Narayana Vasudeva.

Sri Krishn Govind Hare Murare,
So great is this attraction to You oh Lord, that all attachments are
quickly torn.
Fast I enter into Your reign, the light of the Lord, and then I'm truly
born...Hey Nath Narayana Vasudeva.

Sri Krishn Govind Hare Murare,
How can beings that count and measure estimate the immeasurable
bliss that is beyond bounds.
How can I enumerate the virtues and brilliance of You the Creator
himself of these – it astounds...Hey Nath Narayana Vasudeva

Sri Krishn Govind Hare Murare,
I am born from You, You are the source of all, You are the Alpha
and the Omega.
I am in You, You are in me, You are the witness of all creation -
Your amazing Maya...Hey Nath Narayana Vasudeva

Sri Krishn Govind Hare Murare,
You, within whom the whole universe resides, remain formless,
    infinite, eternal, and uncreated.
Being ever liberated you liberate, in ecstatic Bhakti the Bhakt
    merges into You, my Beloved...Hey Nath Narayana Vasudeva

Sri Krishn Govind Hare Murare,
For the Gopis you brought Vaikunta to Vrindavan, You made life
    a celebration!
Where ever I see there is only You, I bow to your ocean of creation...
    Hey Nath Narayana Vasudeva

Sri Krishn Govind Hare Murare,
Only from the heart can You be seen, not the eyes of the mind, nor
    by those in haste.
Rise up! Rejoice! Let's sing His glory, fill knowledge with nectar,
    and become chaste...Hey Nath Narayana Vasudeva

Sri Krishn Govind Hare Murare,
Glory to You O my Lord Krishn! May these tears of love and
    gratitude forever roll from my eyes.
Your devotee begs You not to go and leave me again; can I not be
    forever in your presence...Hey Nath Narayana Vasudeva

Sri Krishn Govind Hare Murare Hey Nath Narayana Vasudeva"

I want to sing to You or say something but my lips do not move, still our
hearts beat in rhythm, our souls communicate. In these moments that seem
eternal, I have truly lived. Then You say to me, "I live forever in your
heart," and disappears into eternity.

Rukha sukha hai ye sansar, jab tak mile na Govind ka pyar (I)
Jeevan ki dhara Radha ban jaae, Kanha se mil kar ek ho jaae (II)
Mein to thi tadap se pyasi, Kaahaan hai o mere Swami (I)
Ab mil gaye antaryami, ab magan hui ye dasi (II)

> *Koi na Bandhu Koi na Sakha sab hai yahan Svarthi Re*
> *Baandh le Preetam se tu Jodhi Vohi hai Saccha Sarthi Re*
> *Dhondha Ras to Paae Peedha Sookha har Sansari Re*
> *Chhod de bandhan arre Kesari tere to Giridhari Re*

I've started singing in conversation with Him. Merging into the rhythm I swing drunk with ecstasy and longing in the heart. Oh, Lord! My mind is filled with your name, and my heart captured by Thee. I feel the rapture of the union of heart, mind, and soul, intoxicated I am with the nectar of bliss. The rhythm of the song of devotion has now taken over me. I have lost my mind and I'm swirling in the ocean of bliss.

"*Karo mann Nanda Nandana ko dhyaan*". "Oh mind; fill yourself with the name of the Lord." This whole world is of no support to me; I come to rest in Thy arms. Oh mind, fill yourself with His name. I roam thirty times and am tired here and there; I have come to rest in Thy arms. May my mind always be filled with Him. May my heart be captured by His presence. I dance in a trance filled with ecstasy as if the whole world doesn't exist. Leave me alone filled with His name. This soul, this bliss, this oneness is all there is. "Karo mann Nanda Nandana ko dhyaan."

I have thrown away that veil of separation, oh Govind. Come to see me again, I will not refuse to see your face this time. You are my only companion. I remember Your most charming, enigmatic face, which I saw and lost my senses. I witnessed the charm, the attraction, and the warmest most handsome face in the entire universe. Eye to eye we saw each other unmoved despite the pouring rain and thunder. Unmoved you were holding the mountain, O Giridhari. Unmoved I was surrendered to you, merged into your eyes eternally, untouched by everything, unaware of the world. That day I realized what I had missed all my life. Had I removed my veil and seen you the first time when you asked to see my face, I would not have lost all these years in this delusion. This moment alone is real in your presence. O Giridhari! You are the only support of Govardhan, we only imagine ourselves also supporting with our little sticks. O Govind! You alone are uplifting my existence, you are my only support.

Ye mann buddhi bhi hai prabhu kripa se.
Ye jeevan bhi hai prabhu kripa se.
Jeevan dhara bhi hai prabhu kripa se.
Jaisi hoon mein prabhu kripa se...unki sharan mein hoon unki kripa se.
Chit saagar ki chhoti si boondh hoon mein Prabhu kripa se.
Apna lein mujhe apni kripa se.
Yeh prem bhakti Prabhu kripa se.
Mein hun nahi bus Unki kripa hai.
Kesari ka pranaam aur samarpan Aap ki kripa mein.

ये मन बुद्धि भी है प्रभु कृपा से
ये जीवन भी है प्रभु कृपा से
जीवन धारा भी है प्रभु कृपा से
जैसी हूँ में प्रभु कृपा से... उनकी शरण में हूँ उनकी कृपा से
चित् सागर की छोटी सी बूँद हूँ मैं प्रभु कृपा से
अपना लें मुझे अपनी कृपा से
यह प्रेम भक्ति प्रभु कृपा से
में हूँ नहीं बस उनकी कृपा है
केसरी का प्रणाम और समर्पण आप की कृपा में

Translation:

This mind and intellect is by His grace.
This life is also by His grace.
The flow of life is also by His grace.
The way I am is by His grace...at His feet by His grace.
A drop in the ocean of consciousness by His grace.
Make me yours by Your grace.
This love and devotion is by His grace.
I am not - only His grace.
Kesari's *pranaam* and surrender into your Grace.

2

My Story

In the most restful states of my heart, I am with You oh Krishna!
Fill me with Your presence.
Smiling as you always do, I am mesmerized by Your presence oh
Krishna! Fill me with Your fragrance.
You are naughty and smart, I am enchanted with Your heart oh
Krishna! Fill me with Your love.
Escape you shall not nor separate from my being oh Krishna! Unite
me with Your being
Oh Krishna! Hare Krishna! Hare Hare.

From Lakshmi I have always received unending love, and to Krishn I have always offered all my love. So my circle of love is complete.

Love has always been the most important aspect of my life. It is that which I seek and that which I am, and it is that which is my life purpose. To understand this more clearly it is important to know a soul's journey. Each one of us has a story which is unique and intriguing. Before I proceed further it is important to narrate mine.

My father's name was Krishn Kant Dubey. His grandfather, Surya Prasad Dubey, was a Krishn devotee and had built a beautiful Dwarkadheesh temple across his *Haveli* (mansion) in Kannauj. My grandmother often narrated the story of my father's birth. She said that the Dwarkadheesh temple bells tolled as he was born the night of Janamashtami (Krishn's birthday). My mother's name is Hem – the name of Lakshmi - and she truly has the personality of Maa Lakshmi. In this house of Dwarkadheesh and to these parents I chose to be born. It was in the mid-sixties, on October seventeenth, a week before Diwali, in Kanpur, near the banks of the Ganges that I was born.

We moved to Delhi when I was around three. I never liked wearing dresses. My mother used to put on a frock on me but I used to pull it off and wear my brother's clothes. She used to get so get upset with me because she wished so much that I would be feminine like her. But I wanted to be like Krishn; in fact, I used to tell her, "I am Krishn!"

15

I loved carrying a *bansuri* (flute), like Krishn, and was in love with Krishn ever since I can remember. Once we went to an art exhibition by "Hare Rama Hare Krishn", in Karol Bagh; I must have been around seven. I went into a trance, transposed, looking at a painting of Gopala stealing butter with the help of his friends. I still remember that painting today, and have a copy of it in my home now.

We lived near Talkatora Gardens in Delhi. Once Satya Sai Baba had come there for an event. My mother took me with her to see him. I remember the masses of people, but nothing of what he said. I saw him sitting on the stage; in fact I kept seeing him sitting on the stage, blessing people by waving his hand, even after people started leaving. My mother pulled me by the hand to go. "But," I said, "He's still sitting there on stage. Why are people leaving?" My mother was rather startled and thought I was mistaken. I wasn't, I could clearly see him there, and how come she couldn't? I think that was quite enough for her and we were off to home.

This wasn't the last time I saw Sai Baba when others couldn't. His presence and miracles continued in my life and still do to this day. That's why I don't like to start on this topic, else things start happening, so let's switch subjects!

In 1975, we left for Zambia, Africa. My father was a surgeon, and very adventurous. He had studied and worked in England before returning to India. He wasn't really happy in India and wanted to go abroad again. This assignment in Africa seemed very exciting so he took it up. We lived in Lusaka, the capital, for a few years and then my father joined the British Copper Mining company and moved to Luanshya. We had a beautiful house that my mother took good care of, and my parents were very fond of gardening. It was a laid back lifestyle in this small town.

I remember a friend of ours had gone to India and my mother had asked them to get some things from there. One of these was a sandalwood statue of Krishn that my mother was going to gift someone. I fell in love with it the moment I saw it and had to have it, so I took it from my mother's hands and said it was mine. My mother was good at singing and listened to bhajans often. I used to also listen in her company and especially loved Krishn bhajans. Sometimes I used to close the door of my room, put on my favorite Krishn bhajans, look at Krishnji's statue, and twirl, and dance in a trance. Once the statue seemed to come alive and I felt it was Sri Krishn himself. I asked him to show me a sign and he did. I was so in love with Krishnji, I felt he was my true companion.

The schools were degrading in Zambia and my parents decided to send me to boarding school in India. In March of 1979 I joined St. Mary's Convent in Nainital, popularly known as 'Ramnee'. So we are 'Ramneeites'. It is located in the beautiful foothills of the Himalayas, established as a 'hill station' by the British. The jewel of Nainital is the lake in the valley, with a road around its perimeter and the town extends up on all sides up from the lake. It's an old school established by British missionary nuns back in 1878. This is an all-girls catholic boarding school and it looks something like Hogwarts from Harry Potter.

My parents had not come to India to drop me off. My father's elder brother, whom we call 'Baa', and my aunt, whom we call, 'Amma', are like parents to us. They had lived in Kanpur for a very long time and it has been a base for us as we moved around the world. They had arranged my admission and came to drop me off in Nainital. I was packed a 'hold-all', which is like a super-sized sleeping bag, with my bedding; and a trunk with all my uniforms and supplies. I was a very shy child and had become even more of an introvert in Africa. My first day in Ramnee was frightful. Not only was it a new school, but also another country, and another culture.

It was my first night in the dorms. The restrooms were called 'Maxes' in Ramnee's slang. We had to wash up before going to bed. We had a plastic basin we filled with cold water from a common sink, then placed it on the long wooden tables in the washing room. While everyone was busy washing up, I was still trying to figure out how to go about it. I filled some water in the tumbler, then continued to brush my teeth and spat in the basin. When I looked down at the dirty water I realized that I couldn't wash my face! That was my first night, and till today, I follow the same regimen of first washing my face and then brushing my teeth.

The change in the school curriculum was very tough for me. I had not done any Hindi, or Indian history, geography, and so on, for many years coming from Zambia. I remember I started by getting zeros in my Hindi tests. It was rather traumatic being away from my parents, not to mention that my poor mother was dying of anxiety and worry back in Africa. There were no emails, texts, messaging, or even frequent phone calls. They called just once when my mom had a bad dream and booked a trunk call to talk to me. The girls were very friendly, happy and giggly. I seemed to like being back with my own people, in the culture I was born in. In Africa I had faced racism and ridicule being a brown skinned Indian. I had developed a strange English accent in Zambia and the girls used to love hearing it, especially hearing me sing "Saturday Night Fever" songs that were very popular that year. I had no clue about the Indian movies and actors they talked about, nor anything Indian.

It was Easter Sunday, April 15, 1979. I was 13 years old. It was night time, and since it was a holiday we didn't have our regular study hour. Instead, it was free time and the study hall had music playing and girls socializing. Gina Gulati and I were having a very philosophical discussion, about infinity,

God, etc. We stepped outside the study hall to the veranda. I told Gina, "I wonder if there is a state of mind without thoughts". It was an interesting thought! So standing on the veranda, we proceeded to the experimentation of eliminating all our thoughts. Yes, we were thirteen! Out in the distance were the shadows of the hills and glimmering lights from homes here and there. I decided to focus on one of those lights while observing my thoughts and focusing on the gap between the thoughts. Initially the thoughts were quite loud and obvious. Slowly the thoughts became more subtle. There were thoughts about thoughts, "Ah! That was a thought". Then came just an observation of the subtlest thoughts. Finally, there was only one thought; the last thought was "I".

And then, suddenly all the music playing inside sucked into my ears, so did my vision, and everything went blank.

And what seemed like a moment later, I felt Gina tapping me on my shoulder. She told me that it's time to head to the dorms. "But", I said, "We just came!" "No", she said, "An hour has passed". It felt like a blink of an eye. I was just standing there, still blanked out and very still. Many years later I realized and was told that I had gone into Samadhi, a deep state of meditation.

So we started walking down from the veranda onto the gravel towards the bathrooms before we went up to the dorms. I was walking beside Gina. The moon was behind us and our shadows in front. A bright light circled my shadow and my shadow disappeared. Then slowly the shadow came back. Gina stopped walking, stunned. I seemed unperturbed and consoled her, not remembering what I told her, though she looked at me aghast! Gina was still shaking but we had to continue walking to the maxes, and then to the dorms. In the dorm we went into a corner and she asked me what's going on! It was a bit too much for her, "Shouldn't we tell Sister?" she asked. I said, "No need." I was fine, in fact in bliss, and felt like I was just observing everything, even my own body, from a very aloof state. I had no retention of thought, everything was just flowing through me, and I felt like a hollow bamboo. It seemed as though someone was talking through me and I told Gina, "I have become a preacher now." That made Gina freak out even more so I stopped talking, and then she couldn't take it anymore so she left quite disturbed.

This state continued for several weeks or months, I can't quite remember. It was like witnessing everything as a movie or a dream. I could tell what people were thinking. I felt enormous power and felt I could even fly if I wanted to. Well perhaps that wouldn't be a good idea but I experimented a little bit to see if it was true. We were practicing for Sports Day and in the upper field I threw a shot-put and it flew across many feet. The girls who were sitting and watching on the hillside got up amazed and shocked. I decided I better keep a low profile. Perhaps some amount of my mind was still there because I couldn't understand what was happening with me and didn't know what to do, I had no Guru, no guidance, and I was very young. I felt alone and no one would understand me, nor could I talk to anyone about what I was experiencing.

I decided that I had to renounce that state and go back to being a "normal" thirteen-year-old girl. This was a bad choice, I wish I had not left that state.

Till today I don't quite know what that light was that came and made my shadow disappear. I have some theories and clairvoyants have given different explanations. Sal Rachele (a clairvoyant) told me that it was Jesus Christ (Sananda) who gave me a visitation to trigger the spiritual awakening in this life. Jesus has a very strong presence in my life even today. There must be a connection.

From the time this event happened, I used to sit up in bed at night and meditate. Sometimes I used to look at the painting of Jesus on the wall of the dorm at night and imagine myself in His lap as a child. It was a very comforting, loving feeling. I never had any method or initiation into meditation at that time, it used to just happen spontaneously. Remember I was thirteen, so still quite pristine, the veil was thin, I was innocent, and the layers of conditioning and mud hadn't accumulated yet. I often say that I was more evolved when I was younger. I was in a natural state of dispassion, of bliss, of witness-hood.

Sports Day was held each summer and this was my first year. I was a sprinter in the 100 and 200-meter races and I ran for the Red House. There were four houses for sports competitions. I loved sports and loved being fast. I remember learning how to march, and one day our vice-captain, Sunita Rana, pulled me aside to instruct me on how to march correctly. She is from Nepal, a beautiful angelic soul, very graceful, and charming. Someone asked her if we were sisters and I was rather flattered! She was one of my role models in Ramnee. In one of the following years, Sunita played Eliza Dolittle in our school's stage adaptation of 'Pygmalion'. This is a play by George Bernard Shaw, and Gina Gulati played the protagonist, Henry Higgins. I remember the last conversations I had with Sunita was at the railway station when we were heading home for the holidays.

After sports day came the mid-terms. As I was struggling in school because of the change in curriculum from Africa, I used to sit on my desk in the study hall during our free time. Anuradha Saluja (Anu) used to see me in distress, and out of the kindness of her heart, she approached me one day to help me out. She is a happy, friendly person, and a very dear soul. Over the course of that year we became best friends. In the years to follow a very deep and long friendship developed that extended to both our families and continues till today. Her cousin, Ruchi Saluja, also studied at Ramnee and was in the same class as us. My friendship with Ruchi also grew over the years and we have shared our lives to this day.

Vinita Dubey

During adolescence one needs guidance, there is so much going on in that teenage brain that leads to confusion. My class teacher was Ms. Rebecca Flynn, and I was very fond of her. She was from the Nainital hills; a quiet, reserved and wise person. I used to talk to her often after class and ask her so many questions. She was so kind to nurture me at that tender age and was a big influence in my life. I think our whole class liked her very much. I kept in touch with her for many years after I left Ramnee. I wish I could find out where she is now.

Our school year was from March to November. Nainital, being in the foothills of the Himalayas, gets snowed, so we went home for the winter months. In the first year itself I developed a closeness with Ramnee, a belongingness, and developed good friends. It was boring to go home. I didn't have many friends in Luanshya. Anu and I used to write long letters to each other almost daily, and my parents used to wonder how we could have so much to say every day!

It was so wonderful going back to Ramnee after the vacations. Again, it was very much like the Harry Potter movies. We used to climb into the trains from our hometowns, with our hold-alls and trunks, head to Kathgodam, the last train stop at the base of the hills, before the trudge up the winding hilly road to our destination, Nainital.

There are many memories from Nainital; the horrible food, the ghost stories, the nuns like Sister Jos – who's an emblem of Ramnee. We always remember the rules we broke, like reading under the blanket with a flashlight. Or when we used to eat food someone brought from home, in the maxes at night and then get caught. The earthquake one year was quite eventful and scary. The ghost stories were the best. Some brave girls went to the graveyard one night after our annual fall play. This night was the start of our Dussera and Diwali holidays, so there was generally a lot of activity, with parents taking their kids home, and the nuns getting busy, so it lends an opportunity to sneak out and do some mischief. I don't think they saw any ghosts, it was pretty freaky though. I know this may sound a little chilling but I will narrate it anyway. Fast forward to now - I had taken a past life regression session some years ago, and in that session I saw myself as a nun, which came with a knowing that I was a nun in Ramnee. I didn't remember her name but have a feeling that this is one of the reasons I went back to Ramnee in this life. What is eerie is that I must have died in Ramnee and my grave is still there.

I decided to leave Ramnee after class 10, and so did Anu. There was a long lapse between the time I left Ramnee and when I re-established contact with my friends from Ramnee. With the advent of Facebook and WhatsApp, we recently got in touch with each other again, and what fun it is to regress to the teenagers we once were in Ramnee!

Back in Zambia, I started preparing for my British 'O' Level exams and my father applied for junior college 'A' Levels for me in what was then Rhodesia. What happened then is that the independence war broke out in Rhodesia and plans had to be changed. I continued with my 'O' Levels that year and started considering going to an International School in India, after which I would go to college in England. Soon after I came back to Zambia my brother, Shagun Dubey, left for the UK to pursue his 'A' levels.

My mother was a Satya Sai Baba devotee and we used to go to Ndola on Sundays for the Bhajan Satsang (*Kirtan*). They were really mesmerizing. There were numerous reports of Baba's *vibhuti* (ash) manifesting in Baba's photos, along with other miracles of healing, visions, and so on. I used to love the energy of the Satsangs, used to get a high from the singing, so I went with my mother. In one of the Satsangs, towards the end, I saw a subtle form of Sai Baba emerge from the stage and walk down the aisle while blessings people on both sides of the aisle with his right hand. It's very interesting, that never in my life, have I ever been startled, scared, or shocked. I usually go into a higher state of consciousness, and just witness what is going on, with an inner knowing. There is no questioning or thinking, just a 'being'.

During the fall of that same year, 1981, I went back to India to visit some International Schools with the help of Amma and Baa. After a few months in Kanpur with them, I heard from my father that he had applied for admission to a US college and that I needed to come back to Zambia to take the entrance exams. I was quite taken aback because I didn't want to go to America. I didn't hold the US in high esteem in terms of moral values and argued with my dad that I didn't want to go there. I don't remember the conversation, but at that point there weren't too many choices for me.

I didn't want to go to the UK either because, after reading Indian history and how the British had exploited India, I had developed a dislike for them.

So it was decided that I would go to the US for college. I remember crying at night and asking God why He was sending me to such a place. I really wanted to stay in India but nothing was working out. I prayed to Krishn and Shirdi Baba. I remember connecting with Shirdi baba eye to eye when I saw his photo and him coming alive. What is interesting is that he did. I started my journey back to Zambia with a train trip from Kanpur to Delhi. We were at the Kanpur train station. Baa and his personal assistant, Satish, left the car to go and find a coolie and reconfirm the reservation. I was alone in the back seat of the car. Just then a *fakir* popped through the front door window wearing dirty old white clothes, a white bandana on his head, and holding a stick in his hand. This time I was taken aback! He started saying things and I was a little scared and shocked so I didn't register everything he said. I thought he was a beggar and would ask for money. What he said was rather amazing. He spoke in Hindi and said something to the effect of… don't worry I am always with you wherever you may go, you will be fine and my blessings are with you…and other things I don't remember. Then he took his head out and I was still in a daze. I looked out of my window and couldn't see where he went. It was much later that I realized that this person was perhaps Shirdi baba who came to console me because I was deeply troubled about going to America.

I started at State University of New York (SUNY), Plattsburg, in August of 1983. My father's class fellow from medical school lived here and became my local guardian. I was a foreign student and made friends with several other foreign students from Asia. There was one person in my psychology class, Ken Cavanaugh, who also became a friend. Ken was a born again Christian and was part of an Evangelical group in college. I somehow got involved in that group and often went to their congregations, attended church and their assemblies in various places. There was a boy, Jonathan, with long curly hair who played the guitar well and sang. I used to also feel so much devotion in their company and loved Jesus as much as they did. I remember my favorite Christian song then was Psalm 23, "The Lord is my Shepherd", sung by Keith Green. I read the Bible and loved Revelations, as I like mystical knowledge. The teachings of the Bible resonated naturally with me. I remember feeling the immense love of Jesus while immersed in this Evangelical community. They somehow thought I would convert! Well, I tried explaining to them that as a Hindu I am free to accept wisdom from all sources and free to love Jesus as an Avatar of God. I don't need to convert for this. Ken, however, believed that physical conversion was still needed to save one's soul and not converting to Christianity would result in going to hell. The only concept that didn't sit well with me is when they kept saying we are sinners and Jesus died to redeem us from our sins. Hinduism always says that we are Brahman, a spark of the divine, and innately positive, not sinners. Our Karm and our conditioning covers this divine aspect of ourselves. The concept that each one is equally God didn't sit well with them, nor did they understand the principle of enlightenment. So there were some differences between the current day Christianity and my Hindu beliefs, but what was common was devotion; it was the same phenomenon for them and me. Loving others and loving God is common in all faiths.

In my second year of college, I moved into an apartment with a Pakistani friend, Shireen Burki. Her father was from a known family in Pakistan and her mother was Irish. She was quite free spirited but a private person. We shared many spiritual conversations. I remember sometimes while talking to her on spiritual subjects, answers and knowledge would just flow through me, things I didn't know and learned as I spoke. Sometimes even my voice would change as though someone else was speaking through me. I used to feel scared and would stop it. This experience of knowledge flowing through me and a higher force speaking through me continued, and I have always shut it down when it starts arising. Shireen also shared her understanding of Islam with me. One Ramadan I fasted the whole month even though she kept it only a few days.

My location guardian in Plattsburgh, Dr. Gulati, had a niece also studying in the same university. She became good friends with me and we used to work together in the computer lab. She was a senior and had recently got engaged. Her fiancé was a Sai Baba devotee. One weekend we were both working in the lab and were talking about Sai Baba. Suddenly I smelt the scent of *vibhuti* coming from my hands. I also felt something flowing from my hands. On a closer look I saw *vibhuti* coming from my hands. I wiped my hands on a cloth and more *vibhuti* kept flowing from my hands. It wouldn't stop! My friend was so shocked and perplexed that she called her fiancé to ask what to do. She had me speak to him as well. Finally I closed my eyes and consciously made an intention to have this stop. And it did. Phew!

The following year I moved in with some Malaysian girls. They were quiet, shy, well-mannered, gentle, simple, humble, innocent and religious Muslims. One of them, Ada, became my best friend. I started reading the Holy Quran and learning about Islam from them. I also learned the Namaz from Ada and learned the first Surah by heart.

One semester I took a course in Comparative Religions and loved it. This was truly my calling, seeing the commonness amongst all wisdom traditions. After class, some of us used to have conversations on the different religions, and I remember emphasizing the spiritual aspects of each. During my free time, I used to love spending time in the library reading books by various spiritual masters, Swami Vivekananda being my favorite. I could relate to all the deeper aspects of consciousness through an inner remembering. The realization happened as I read the words that had flowed from the higher consciousness of these spiritual masters.

Another semester I had taken a course in philosophy and religious studies in which I did a lot of research on the changing versions of the Bible from the Aramaic to Hebrew, Greek, Roman and then English. I had long conversations with my professor who asked me to write to a library in London that stored the research by Isaac Newton on the Bible. I discovered the amazing studies Newton did on the Bible, especially on the Apocalypse, which was also of great interest to me. His research proved that the Greek version of the Bible was corrupted to introduce the Trinity (John 5:7) and altering the stature of Jesus from man to God (1 Timothy 3:16). Newton kept this a secret because it would be considered blasphemy. This research was published as "A Historical Account of Two Notable Corruptions of Scripture" about 25 years after Newton died. Isaac Newton was a member of a secret society known as the Priory of Sion; he left behind a trove of amazing manuscripts on the occult studies of the Bible that he shared with no one and were discovered after his death. This was the start of my interest in the occult, the secrets held by a few that revealed the hidden truths.

One of my favorite courses in college was on the Art and Architecture of India. I love temples in general and especially south Indian temples. There were so many amazing facts about these temples such as the science and mathematics behind the *Vastu Shastra* – the ancient Vedic knowledge on architecture. After taking this course I traveled to India during the summer and went on a tour of South India with Amma and Baa, and visited several ancient temples there.

The last summer of college I went to the extension of the Sringeri Shankaracharya Peetham in Pennsylvania. I was a counselor for a group of children during their summer camp. We also learned many Vedic chants, rituals, and knowledge. I learned the complete Vedic *puja* ritual and was in charge of the Ganesh temple. I had to do the sunrise and sunset prayer ritual daily and loved it. The main temple deity was Sri Rajarajeshwari. Each *Peetham* has five deities; Guru, Ganesh, Lakshmi-Narayan, Shiv-Shakti, and Saraswati. The main temple had a statue of Sri Krishn and I used to sit next to him. One day, as I was leaving the hall after a session, I was overcome with an intense attraction and calling from Sri Rajarajeshwari. I turned around and looked at her and she seemed alive and very powerful. I ran to her, dropped to my knee, and started crying profusely. I was overcome with intense feelings of longing, devotion, and gratitude, all at the same time. A part of me was still wondering what was happening to me, but the greater part of me had surrendered. There were only a few in the hall, mainly Swamis, who fell into silence and whispered to leave me alone. That night I dreamt of an Indian woman in a red sari, with gold ornaments, dancing. Perhaps that was a *darshan* of the Divine Mother.

There was a Swami there who used to channel a group of beings called, "The Circle of Seven." Several people went to him for a reading but I wasn't interested, and a bit scared too. The head Swami insisted that I have a session so I went. It was a strange experience of hearing the Swami's voice change and hearing other entities speak through him. I asked them what happened to me when I was thirteen. After a long pause, they told me that it was a state of perfection that I had invoked. They went on to tell me that

I had a deep love for Krishn (which I did not tell them), that I would marry soon, and that they would talk to me after many years once some Karma was done. They told me several other things about my nature and gave guidance on what I should work on.

After I graduated from college I went back to live with Amma and Baa in Kanpur and worked at IIT, Kanpur. I got married a year and a half later in Kanpur. After I got married we then moved to the US where he was working as an IT consultant. Over the years we had two lovely sons, both born in Chicago. I was fully ingrained in worldly life and social engagements. Some in-laws also lived close to us in Chicago. Certain negative influences affected our marital relationship. The Chicago years were probably the worst time of my life. After nine years in Chicago, we moved to the San Francisco bay area, and I was relieved though the detrimental factors continued to affect my marriage.

In 1999, I heard about the Art of Living Foundation's spiritual course from a friend, Madhu Dhillon. She explained it to be a course in which one learns breathing techniques. At that time I was looking for some meditation courses, spiritual communities, and higher knowledge. I thought this to be an entry level course and suggested to someone in my family that he take it, which he did. After seeing the transformation in him, I decided to take it shortly thereafter. So I took my first Art of Living course in September 1999 in Milpitas, CA. The technique taught in the course is quite powerful and I also liked the knowledge they shared. I was on a fast track after that, taking the advanced course and enrolling in knowledge sessions to learn some ancient Vedic texts. I went for the Guru Purnima celebrations in 2000 and that's when I first met Sri Sri Ravi Shankar. There were not that many people at the time, and access to him was much easier. Over the years I became very active in the Art of Living Foundation, organizing courses, events, getting involved in service activities and programs, and eventually getting trained as a teacher and teaching. I had several personal experiences with Sri Sri, some of them profound. My formal initiation into meditation was given by a senior Art of Living teacher, Philip Fraser. This is an ancient Vedic tradition whereby the teacher gives the student the blessing and technique to meditate. There are different techniques, the one that Art of Living follows is based in the Shakti tradition, whereby a '*Beej*' (seed) Mantra is given. It's quite fascinating how a Mantra is chosen for a student. This Mantra is kept secret by the student to retain its power. When Philip initiated me, he gave me some instructions on meditation and then observed me meditate over three days. As I had been meditating since I was a teenager using my own modality, using this new method was an effort. Philip observed that I was not transcending the mind, as my mind was still making the subtle effort to take the mantra and follow the instructions. So on the second day I decided to go back to my own practice and meditate. This time I went very deep and he noticed it. I told him that I just did what I've been doing since I was young. I also told him that many times while I've meditated, as my thought go to null, my mind blanks, and also my breath arrests. And then when I come back to consciousness, as my mind starts getting thoughts, my breath returns. He said that the breath can't stop, perhaps it becomes very subtle, but I was quite sure, that during that span of time when I was "gone", there was no thoughts, or breath.

In addition to the meditation course, I took many other courses in the Art of Living, and during the Art of Living courses I had many transformational experiences. I had also taken the past life regression, which is a Yogic method to remove past life impressions, and I did see some past lives, one in particular. It was a very powerful experience for me that brought up a deep wound, and released it. I also had an out of body experience, and felt the presence and grace of Guruji during and after the process. He is my Guru and I have learned much from him. Guruji has done a tremendous amount in uplifting millions of people around the globe; it has brought them in touch with their own divinity, made them more spiritual, and helped them heal and evolve.

From the time I was a teenager I had a deep yearning to realize the truth, and read several texts of Vedic knowledge with commentaries from great luminaries like Swami Vivekananda. I wanted to do a deep dive into the study of *Shastras* (Vedic texts) and so I embarked on a study of the Bhagavad Gita and Upanishads through Chinmaya Mission, San Jose, CA. The local Swamiji here, Swami Prabodhananda, was brilliant and I was truly blessed to learn from him. I also got several DVDs with commentaries by Swami Chinmayananda and Swami Tejomayananda (the current head of Chinmaya Mission) on various texts. There were times I was studying two or three texts in one day simultaneously. The knowledge came very naturally and easily to me, so it wasn't a strain. It powered in like a deluge in a short span of two years. For me, there is an inner awakening, realization, recognition, opening up and enlivening, as I read. It's not a mere academic or theoretical exercise. Many people study so much and it becomes an intellectual gain alone. Then it's not knowledge or wisdom, it's simply information. My purpose is to awaken, so in everything I am seeking to realize the ultimate truth. After this period of learning and realization is when I wrote my first book, "Eternal Way to Bliss".

In December 2012, my marriage separation began, though not initiated by me. There were many threats before but now it was serious. In January of 2013, I spoke to a medium, Kevin Ryerson, who channeled several beings including an ancient Egyptian temple priest, Ahtun Re. I asked about my marriage, and he said that it would end in about two years when my younger son is off to college, and that's exactly what happened. He also told me that it would be for my good, as the Karmic balance would close and a better part of my life would begin, which he described. I had also asked about a previous life of which I had many visions and had also seen in an Art of Living past life regression. I felt I was reliving that life, that it was the same spouse and in-laws. He did confirm this. I value the insights he gave me on my soul path, my life purpose and the role I play in creation. The ability to raise people's consciousness through meditation on sacred sounds is something other clairvoyants also mentioned independently. 2013-2014 were transition years of my life into a new phase. I had also brought my mother here to live with us because she couldn't manage alone after my father's passing. The grace of the divine was to plan to have my mother here with her unconditional loving support as I moved through the most difficult phase of my life – marital separation.

I felt such a relief after our separation, like a bird that had been freed from a cage, as free as the breeze blows. For others it was a tragedy and for me a blessing in disguise. It was also a lesson to love and accept myself as I am, and to have self-worth.

Vinita 2.0

After September of 2014, I felt a new chapter of my life open up. New knowledge started descending on me and coming at me from all directions like a deluge, a crash course to prepare me for the next phase of my life ahead. I had been told by Ahtun Re and my Shaman that my role in creation was to serve others by raising their consciousness through sound vibrations. So I delved into learning about this area. It was like diving into a deep and vast ocean; the knowledge was so fascinating that I could not stop devouring more and more. I have written about some of my findings at the end of the chapter on "Anjali – A divine offering". I learned that most ancient spiritual traditions and cultures had a common theme regarding sound vibrations and it's manifestation in sacred geometry. I have the advantage of knowing the Vedic knowledge and could bridge what these new scientific findings say with the ancient Vedic knowledge. There are far too many deep secrets that are revealed to the soul appropriately at each stage of evolution to the soul – the knowledge is never ending.

In one of the videos I was watching by Gregg Braden on vibrations, there was another completely unrelated section inserted. Suddenly it started talking about "The Pleiadian Message" channeled by Barbara Marciniak, regarding the awakening about to happen and the transition to a new golden age. The message was so profound that I could not fathom it at first, and initially I thought it was a science fiction video. Then I went back over it pausing, and repeating, till I could absorb the whole message. It took me a few days to wake up to the fact that this was a message from alien beings channeled by a human. What was astounding is that it rang so true within, as though I knew it deep within, and it was like an awakening from amnesia.

We all have had this experience when we hear words of wisdom, we recognize them within, as if remembering from a forgotten state. This message talked about the vast races that exist in the universe and about the history of the humans on this planet. These beings from the Pleiades star system had been instrumental in the civilization on Earth in our ancient past and had come back to be a catalyst for our awakening. Most importantly they spoke about how we had dropped from our divine state into the darkness of ignorance, and this was done by a dark alien species. These negative alien beings controlled most of the rich and powerful people on the earth and ran their agenda from backstage. They also controlled us through psychological means via media, technology, consumerism, and addictions. It was like the movie Matrix. They said now there is a divine intervention to take us into an inevitable new age. A new dawn is coming to our planet with rapid changes and incredible transformations, and we are the family of light beings who volunteered for this mission to come to this planet and assist humanity through this transition.

I began reading about the Pleiadians, and other beings and my search opened me up to another world of beings, dimensions, and the coming of a new age. I found a huge community of people who wrote and discussed this across the globe. All this was as though it was held from me till now, and it was time that I step into it. Now I find more people being exposed to this with the internet carrying everyone together in a collective wave. These writings connected the ancient past of the earth with the present and future. The history of the universe and earth that I read from channeled messages was quite different from that in our history books. Lemuria, Atlantis, ancient Egypt, Greece, Bharat (India), were all civilizations of highly evolved beings from other star systems. There were many star races that engineered the DNA of the native human race.

In one of my searches, I found a chapter of Sal Rachele's book online. As soon as I started reading it, there was instant resonance with me. I started reading the book from the start and was glued to it till I finished it. It is his book titled, *"Earth Changes and 2012"*. I went to his website and signed up for a personal session with Sal. I had so many questions to find out who I am, what my life purpose is, about my past, present and future. It was a fascinating session to say the least. He saw people and things so clearly, without any way for him to know. It was also very helpful and beneficial for me to know the cause of things, to understand situations, people, how to handle situations and guidance on what to do. I had several sessions with him every few months when I wanted to get the true picture of people and situations because I can't see the truth behind things yet. Clairvoyance is a gift everyone has, and will come naturally as the soul progresses.

After several months of reading and experiencing many phenomenal things, I found many personalities as the leaders of the new age. There were many conspiracy theories as well. I do not want to get into the details here, but the essence of it was to transform the world that has about seventy-five percent negativity, conflict, competition, and control, to a new higher vibrational positive earth, that is based on and imbibes compassion, cooperation, wisdom and conscious communities. The central theme of the new age message is that most people on earth are solely focused on physical, material aspects that are the three-dimensional reality (3D). Some of these souls would progress towards the fourth dimension (4D), which examines the mind, feelings, and the spiritual aspects of existence. Perhaps twenty-five percent of humanity is already in 4D. A very small percentage would move into the fifth dimension, which is the dimension of light and love. This would be a spiritual ascension, and the soul would transcend the cycle of rebirth.

Relating the Vedic to the New Age

During my readings, I had to relate the new age terminology to the Vedic terminology. When we are familiar with one culture, tradition, or set of terminology we often don't recognize the corresponding term in another and therefore can't relate, or think it's different.

When we are able to find the relationship between definitions then suddenly we realize a lot of commonalities between the ancient, the new, the scientific and the spiritual. It somehow confirms that it must be the truth if so many for so long are saying the same thing.

In this age, we read spiritual terms in English. Then there are ancient terms in Vedic knowledge, in the Jewish Kabbalah, in the Egyptian culture, the Greek, Mayan, and so on. Then there are scientific terms which may correspond with a spiritual aspect.

The terms used in Western or new age spirituality include:

'Ascension', 'Dimensions', 'Beings', 'Extra-Terrestrials', 'Soul', 'Consciousness', and so on.

In Vedic terminology, '*lokhs*' relates to 'dimensions'.

'Beings' and 'extra-terrestrials' relate to the different beings mentioned in the Veds and Purans.

There are fourteen lokhs. Seven are lower or descending lokhs below the physical universe. The other seven higher lokhs include:

'*Bhu*' is the physical three-dimensional universe;

'*Bhuvar*' is the astral realm where souls that have passed on reside, and relates to the fourth dimension;

'*Svar*' or '*Dev*' *lokh* is where the *Devas* and some *Rishis* reside. These *Devi-Devatas* (deities) are beings of light. '*Dev*' means luminous one, or one who illumines. This lokh broadly relates to the fifth dimension.

In these three lokhs, souls recycle from birth to death, called the cycle of '*Samsar*'.

Then there is '*Maha*' (sixth dimension), '*Jana*' (seventh dimension), 'Tapa' (eighth dimension), and highest '*Brahma/Satya*' lokh (ninth dimension), all a part of creation, or greater reality. What we see as the physical universe is only the three-dimensional reality or '*Bhu*' lokh.

All these lokhs are still in the sphere of creation, duality, or *Maya*. Brahman, the Ultimate Supreme Consciousness, transcends this. Time slows down and space expands as we move into higher lokhs or dimensions. These are not physical but subtle realms.

The 'extra-terrestrials' and 'beings' I read about related to the many subtle forms of beings that are mentioned in the Vedic texts. These include the *Devas, Asuras, Rishis, Siddhas, Kinnars, Yakshas, Gandharvas, Manas putras, Prajapatis, Kumaras, Avatars,* and so on. In addition to these subtle forms, there may be physical forms of beings on other planets, like humans. We don't talk about it now in the *Kali Yuga*, but before the *Kali Yuga* other beings, dimensions, higher states of consciousness and special abilities such as telepathy, were common and normal.

Ancient Vedic texts talk about mind-born sons, or subtle thought forms, of *Brahma-ji*, the creator deity. Four of these are the *Kumars*; they never age. Their names are *Sanat Kumar* (who I believe also manifests as *Maha-avatar Babaji*), *Sanandan* (mentioned by several as the over-soul of Jesus), *Sanak*, and *Sanatan*, These mind-born sons of *Brahma* also include the seven original *Rishis*, also called *Prajapatis*, the creator beings. These were not physical forms but thought forms. These beings last as long as creation lasts. Then there are beings that are light forms, *Devas*. Many of these beings (including *Rishis*), came to earth and started the human civilization or mingled with humans for progeny; these stories are in *Purans, Itihaas*, eluded to in the old testament, the Egyptian books, and many other ancient texts. Some physical forms were also organically growing here. A lot of these *Rishis, Devatas, Siddhas, Avatars*, etc. are also capable of taking physical form, i.e., descent from higher dimensions into the third, earth dimension. That's why the *Rishis* and people of ancient civilizations were so advanced in their knowledge. There were far more evolved beings that descended here on Earth and built advanced communities and cultures. Some of the remnants of these ancient civilizations and knowledge can be found in the *Vedas, Kabbalah*, the Old Testament, the Egyptian civilization, and so on.

We are familiar with the blue skinned *Avatars, Sri Ram* and *Sri Krishn*. They were actually blue skinned and the texture was like that of the dolphins. *Avatars* are one of the highest evolved beings in the Vedic tradition, higher than *Devatas*. The Vedic texts also talk about several *Nakshatras*, the main star of a constellation. There are twenty-seven main *Nakshatras*, and one more, *Abhijit*, which is the star Vega. In the *Gita, Bhagavan Sri Krishn* says that among the *Nakshatras* I am *Abhijit*. *Rudra*, the Vedic deity of transformation and transcendence, is associated with *Ardra Nakshatra*, which is the star Betelgeuse, of the Orion constellation. The origins of the Indian race, I have heard, was seeded by beings from Vega/Lyra, and perhaps others including Sirius and Orion. The seven *Rishis* are the seven stars of Ursa Major. Could it be that these subtle light beings were from those stars?

The Vedic texts mention the gradual decline in civilization through the ages, called *Yugas*; this relates to the decline in knowledge, *Dharma* (natural law), dropping from higher states of consciousness, and removal of the light aspect. We are presently in the age of darkness (or ignorance), the *Kali*

Yuga. In this *Yuga,* we are as though in deep slumber, the light has been shut out and because of the lack of light, dark forces are more dominant, such as anger, hatred, greed, and other negative emotions.

Many of us are reincarnations of those same highly evolved beings of the ancient world, the *Rishis, Siddhas, Devatas, Avatars* and other evolved beings. We have completely forgotten our true nature, we have lost our true history, so we think we are inferior beings struggling with darkness. Now we pray to Gods such as *Sri Krishn* and *Sri Ram* and worship the *Rishis* and *Devatas* as though they are separate from us, but they are part of our spiritual lineage. They are great highly evolved divine beings, our guardians, guides and spiritual masters. When consciousness awakens in us and we remember our true nature, then that is the *Avatar* consciousness in us or the Christ consciousness in us. We will remember our history and our connection with the greater universe, the oneness. There will be unity of consciousness among all beings. That consciousness within us is subtle light; it is a higher vibration than the lower vibration of matter. It is like the difference between water vapor and ice. So when this realization and awakening happens in us, there will only be light and, therefore, no darkness. This is like remembering, and going back to what we really are. This is the return of the *Satya Yuga*, the age of truth and purity, as the Yugas are circular.

The new age material talks about the coming of...a new age! This would be assisted by certain galactic waves of high vibration energy. At the present time, a lot of people will evolve to the fourth dimension and become more spiritual. Many are already in the fourth dimension/density prior to this 'shift' into the new age. I have read a lot about 'Ascension', referring to the evolution of a small percentage of people from the fourth dimension to the fifth dimension of love and light; this is the spiritual ascension. For some this would also be followed by a physical ascension, that is, going from carbon-based body cells to silicon based body cells that can conduct light, and becoming a 'being of light' - the next evolutionary species. The *Dev roop* or light being form is of the *Svar/dev lokh*.

New age masters also talk about Gaia (earth) transitioning from the third dimension to the fourth/fifth dimension.

The concept of "*Moksha*" is liberation from the cycle of birth and death, transcending duality into a realization of Oneness, and merging back to Brahman (eternal universal consciousness).

The ascension spiral is the evolutionary path of a soul through the various dimensions back to the Source. Ascension at the current time means evolving to the fifth dimension, spiritually and physically, as discussed earlier. This means going beyond the cycle of birth and death, to the realization of Oneness, and in terms of physical enlightenment, having an immortal light body. There are many variations this basic core new age message.

We live in exciting times. Let see where destiny is leading us!

It's a beautiful endless journey in eternity and infinity. We are like one spec of a fractal, an exact replica of the whole that replicates itself infinitely.

My journey continues to unfold. A passage that lights up as the fog clears, step by step. My soul is in the driver's seat; the ego serves the soul. The soul is treading the path it chose, the mind simply watches. It is like a template that is being activated.

May I be who I truly am – an unlimited, infinite, ray of the Supreme.

I am here for a purpose at this time. May I fulfill my purpose. I am here to serve and love unconditionally. Challenges still remain, perhaps as an opportunity to evolve.

3

Relationships: The Problem Statement

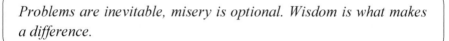

> *Problems are inevitable, misery is optional. Wisdom is what makes a difference.*

One of the biggest challenges in life is handling relationships! If you have mastered relationships you have mastered life. Sri Sri Ravi Shankar says that those who are good with machines are not good or patient with people. I fall in that category. Relationships, relating and connecting with people has been my greatest challenge. It is an aspect of myself that I am consciously working on improving with sincerity. I do love everyone, yet why is it that I continue to face problems in relationships? It's not just me, I see most people struggling with maintaining relationships over long periods of time. Complications arise the closer one becomes.

Sometimes I wonder why people are so complicated. A lot of people are just superficial in their relationships; there's a hypocrisy of sweetness on the outside and bitterness on the inside. Why can't people be transparent? It is good to talk sweetly and be nice, but it should be authentic. Also, while rawness doesn't mean expressing negativity, it's better to clean up the inside before speaking rather than keeping the negative and being a hypocrite. I personally prefer one who shows me their soul, even if hard to take - at least I know what they are, rather than those who keep quiet, or who are fake. When I see different sides of a person that are inconsistent, or when I realize it was a façade or the truth of a person isn't so pretty, I am saddened.

Isn't there anyone in the world I can trust to be genuine? Why can't people be simple and natural? Maybe I should live in a village where people are simple! I know I need to accept everyone as they are, without judgment, though very few have truly purified to love and accept people as they are.

As I confess to not being so good with people, I make a good case to study and share my learning. Though I have progressed over the years, and today my relationships are much better, there's still room for improvement. The mantra that I've learned to practice is to have detachment with compassion. That is the key.

I tell my friend Nirmal Mozumdar, a healer, about my woes and she shares:

"I also fall into this category of not having very good relationships with others around me, but I wouldn't call it bad too. In a way I am becoming more mature, detached, and trying to accept myself unconditionally and when I do so, I make a space in my heart for accepting others also the way they are. It's not an easy job, as the logical, analytic mind is always at work, constantly chattering about the not so good aspects of myself and of others around me. It's a battle within our self. Only by becoming aware and consciously deciding not to fall prey to judgments of good and bad can help one find self-love. And it's the same thing for others. If we are constantly judging people, where is the time or place in our heart for love for them?"

The Art of Living Course point, 'Accept People and Situations as they are', is very useful in understanding the relationship cycle.

The first phase can start from either a negative or a positive perception of the other person. Let's take the positive one. This starts with a honeymoon period. You have just come to know someone and both see all the good things in each other.

As the interactions increase and proceed slowly, one starts noticing the tendencies or characteristics repeatedly in the other person. "Oh! She has a short temper", or "Wow! He has a big ego", and so on. So the negative side starts overshadowing our perception.

Then there are five aspects that affect our relationship that comes from limited awareness, as Deepak Chopra mentions in his book "Spiritual Solutions". It's very important to be 'aware' of these aspects:

* Perceptions
* Beliefs
* Assumptions
* Expectations
* Feelings

And I would add another big one which is *judgments.*

When the cycle turns from the honeymoon period to the not-so-perfect phase, we enter the individual differences phase. Our desires create demands and expectations of the other person. This makes love, and the relationship, conditional. Our likes and dislikes influence our relationships so much. As humans our dislikes (the negative) always dominates our mind and this causes us to react with some negative emotion. All this stems from ignorance, not being established in our own Self.

Sometimes relationships can take a bad turn from here and a lot of heartaches follows. A lot of emotional drama is enacted, hurtful words are spoken, which leaves our minds in a whirlwind and our hearts broken. One is either sad, scared, or becomes mad. The relationship has entered the conflict phase.

If the two people involved can work through this negative stage with love and respect for each other, the relationship can be saved. The cycle will continue with renewed closeness and seeing some positives again in the other person: "She acts stupid sometimes but she doesn't mean it", or "He is arrogant at times but he's a good-hearted guy", and so on. Though impressions have been formed, and patterns are repeated, the relationship will either improve or degrade depending on how much the two people sustain the love and respect for each other.

If only one of the two is willing to work on the relationship, then it becomes an im-balanced relationship. If there is mutual love and respect, then the relationship blossoms, as both will work on accepting and supporting the other person as he/she is rather than demanding and expecting. Respecting also means giving each other space, and love is the closeness of the heart, genuinely caring for the other person. We need to be willing to work on improving the shortcomings in our self, only then can a relationship serve a purpose on our path of growth. When a relationship no longer serves a purpose in our life, it breaks apart. However; when there's mutual growth, the relationship and companionship become stronger and there is a deeper bond, a renewed honeymoon phase! And the cycle continues...

The relationship of love is of the greatest challenge. The emotions of romance. The relationship with a partner. I wish someone would give us training on how to handle these relationships. I was talking to a family lawyer who told me that there was a US poll which found that 80% of couples said that they weren't in a happy marriage. It's hard to live your entire life even with parents, children, or siblings. There are always ups and downs in a relationship, but when the going gets tough and the relationship is on the rocks it is only the inner core of love in both that can save it from breaking apart.

The Institution of Marriage

There are two perspectives, a wife's and a husband's, which are complimentary. The intention is not to demean, demonize, or criticize either side, but to state what is viewed and experienced from either side, and each one has their own perception of reality. Problems creep in when both parties can't resolve attitudes that are affecting the other. What is the basis of a failed relationship? When a spouse has constant expectations and demands stemming from selfishness, it kills the love. Love means to be there for the other person.

Some husbands often feel the need to reduce the worth of the partner to feel good about themselves; this is a natural defense of the ego. Then there's conflict when the wife refuses to be reduced to rubble and maintains her individuality. On the other hand, an ideal husband is one who accepts his partner's individuality, expressing his love by being a supportive partner, as well as accepts and celebrates her strengths.

A good wife is one who cultivates her husband's ego, through loving praise and support, and nurtures him almost like a mother would a son.

No one is perfect, why expect perfection? If we are constantly finding faults and what's negative in the other person, then neither will be happy. Each person has their own opinions, likes, and dislikes. There's no right or wrong. The perception, judgment, bias, and reaction depend upon whether we are there for the other person's happiness or have developed patterns of dislike.

For example, if the wife suggests a place to go on vacation, the husband's immediate reaction is that it's a bad idea because the attitude towards the wife is as such. Now if the children, or his mother, or someone else he loves suggests the same thing, his reception and reaction are open and positive. Haven't we seen this all the time? So it's not about right or wrong, but the love we have for the other person, to make the other person happy.

Several times we have seen that when one spouse commits a minor mistake, the other spouse is very upset, but when their child makes even a major mistake, the parent's love spontaneously excuses the mistake: "Oh! It's OK, he didn't do it on purpose," and so on.

There are many types of failed marriages and relationships. I've seen that it can be from physical, verbal or emotional abuse, aggression, extra-marital relationships, domination, fear, unfairness, difference in values, or just incompatibility of natures. A lot of times I've seen a woman being constantly reprimanded, criticized, demeaned; even publicly, which causes them to lose their self-esteem and confidence and could even lead to a point of mental disability and becoming dysfunctional.

Individuals who are weak-spirited and have a big ego are very complicated as they do a lot of things to cover up their weakness. Depending on the culture and generation, men are conditioned to be a certain way and treat their wives in a particular manner. I have personally heard men praise those women who take abuse passively, accept being inferior, and are subservient. This defines a "good" wife. Some may be hypocrites in showing how liberal they are but in practice they hold the same beliefs that may belong to the dark ages. I have heard men who say, "You don't know how other husbands and in-laws treat their wives; you should be thankful for how nicely you are treated!"

Why do some men abuse their wives? Since a weak man can't express his ego in the world, it results in him showing his authority over his wife to give himself a sense of "being a man". You can't be someone who's incapable of doing much and then demand respect because true respect can only be earned. Just showing ego and arrogance doesn't work. Such men constantly discipline their wife like an army general. Yet they may be scared of saying "no" to their child, even what's good and best for them because they fear the child's reaction, and being disliked hurts the ego. For the same reasons, they are also timid to do or say anything to other people. They would even bear injustice and be used by others, but would not have the guts to speak up. Such people are obviously liked by people because they are constantly pleasing others to win praise which boosts their ego.

Now we are in the twenty-first century. Problems come in when a woman marries a man whose ideology is like that of the sixteenth-century. We need to know how to deal with such a spouse. The reaction of a "modern" woman is that of intolerance to injustice, inequality, ignorance and double standards. How can a man say and do anything he wants, and the wife should just keep shut? For the husband it's unacceptable to see his modern educated wife behaving the way a man would; she would be termed dominating, strong charactered, and breaking the norms. The sixteenth-century ideological husbands expects a traditional wife who is seen and not heard, who spends her entire life in the kitchen, taking care of the children, serving her husband, who never speaks her viewpoint in public, lives her life according to the husband's wishes and kills her own. Won't every man want such a wife? Why not? It serves them well.

A shrewd wife is one who knows how to handle her husband, keep him happy with false praise that boosts his ego, and feeding his weaknesses. Having a husband blinded from their real self, and wrapped around their little finger, they get away by doing whatever they want. An avant-garde woman just speaks back and gets tarnished. Sometimes the truth is harsh and it's not good to speak the truth if it may cause a reaction or hurt the other person. It's important to be more patient, tactful, have more discipline on expression, and that's being wise. It's not what you say, but how and when you say it that's more important.

Why are some women labeled as a rebels? Because they feel that men and women are peers and couples should be friends. As men and women are created equal, there should be no double standards. Today women are doing well in school, go to work and sometimes have a better career than their husbands. At the same time, they take responsibility for the home and children. Why should they then be treated inferior? Why should men disrespect their wives?

So why do husbands and wives stay in a relationship when there is a lack of love and respect, and neither one is happy? Many times it's for the children. A lot of women are not financially independent and feel they would not survive, or won't know how to earn to support themselves, or that their lives would be dysfunctional. Some stay on because of family, cultural and social pressures, of what people would say. But this has changed a lot now. More and more couples are separating and marriage is more of a choice and not "till death do us apart". More women are earning and are quite capable of living alone.

There are many couples who are very happily married. Both have immense love and respect for each other. Not all men are as defined here. I know so many who are amazing husbands and in fact, it's the wife's shortcomings that cause the problems that the husband has to deal with. Women are not perfect by any measure and it's a lot harder for two women to deal with each other because they are more emotional and complicated. However; what is represented here is a segment of what I've seen and experienced. The younger generation especially is moving more towards equality than the male-dominated cultures of the past. There are some matriarchal societies in the world too. A lot of the younger generation isn't even getting married; they prefer non-committal live-in relationships. What is marriage? The ceremonial wedding and a legal transaction that places the label of husband and wife to bear children. The concept of marriage will continue to evolve into more liberal and fluid forms.

No matter how open the definitions become relationships will continue to be complex. So we often expect our partner to be a certain way defined by us, demand that they do certain things, and be the source of our happiness. The other expectation is that of love. In many relationships, we expect love from the other person in return for our love for them. Our desire for love never gets quenched because we are constantly looking for more, want it expressed in a certain way, and want the same amount of love in return. These emotions and desires not only cause pain and drain us but also becomes a burden on the one we love to constantly reciprocate with a manner we expect. Is it not so?

People live in the limitations of their beliefs and definitions of what a woman should or shouldn't be. Sometimes roles are reversed because of personal natures and abilities. A husband can be feminine and weak, a father motherly, but a wife has to be submissive not strong, and a mother can't do things fathers do. There are double standards some question but are not supposed to. That's the way things are, they say, the earlier you accept the better. Then they judge, criticize, and want to change their spouse according to their conditioning. Some adhere by their inculcation of what's conventional and accepted, assuming these are eternal truths. Norms change over the ages and what was wrong in the 16th century is okay today, but still people continue to blame, criticize and judge. Weak and fearful they are of other's opinions, then they force their partner to fit into their subjective definitions of a role. Unwilling they are to see within, they lay the blame on the other.

I will tell a story. There was a woman who lived some centuries ago, and she was different from other people. She didn't follow the norms of an orthodox society and the narrow-minded demands of her in-laws. She was a rebel. She spoke of what was wrong with common practices, but she was a person of principles. She did what she thought was right and didn't compromise on the truth. While others tried to convince her to follow blindly and timidly, she was bold and brave. This caused her to gain the displeasure of her in-laws to a point where they wanted to harm her. She was shunned, a black sheep of the family, unpopular, and outcast from society. Her parents had died and she had no one who loved her unconditionally. She felt so much pain and felt so unloved. She looked for unconditional love like someone dying of thirst and only found the poison of anger and venom of hate, especially from her in-laws. This deep pain and strong impressions of being disliked by people and not being loved lasted a long time. It was the root cause of her patterns in relationships and in dealing with people in the world. She felt no one loved nor understood. Being chastised by people, she closed up, cut off, and became completely introverted. She felt small and insignificant, her self-esteem crucified to a point of extinction. The criticism from others killed the life force within her. She bore so much pain. These projections of her impressions continued to create her reality.

But it was her role in creation to challenge limitations!

Even today I have seen unconventional women suffer emotional abuse for years that suffocates the life force within. Yet that is the acceptable method to contain a free-thinking woman into the narrow channels of what is thought of as right. She is made to feel that she's a horrible person, not a good wife, and a bad mother (which is the most painful and damaging). Despite this untruth, she continues to do her duties to the best of her abilities, and still loves, yet in pain.

So then should a person die again with the guilt hung around her neck of not being a good wife or mother? Does she not have the right to self-expression? Please don't crucify her for being different. If a person is not doing anything immoral or harming anyone, can she not express her own unique personality? If not then she will feel blamed, alienated by society, isolated; it's very traumatic and such impressions last a long time.

I have some advice for the woman who is suffering.

It's better for you to know that it's your role in creation to question the limitations people live within, and this is the treatment you will get for challenging the conformists. So now finally do you get it? If so, then you will move beyond the suffering, from the feeling of not being loved, of being rejected, shunned and labeled as a bad woman. This knowing will free your heart from being locked up under a heavy weight. This is the opportunity to find yourself. Deep within you, in the spine, a seed of love, is in excruciating pain, covered by a hard knotted heart - it finally releases the pain. It blossoms like a flower.

The Rise of the Divine Feminine

Many flowers have been crushed before they could blossom. A flower is soft, gentle, fragrant and beautiful, yet considered weak and irrelevant in a world where physical strength, mind, and ego dominate. When there is dis-balance in nature, there comes suffering and then a correction to re-balance. There are matriarchal and patriarchal cultures in the world, but for a long time now the male dominated cultures have been more prominent.

Women have come to sacrifice themselves for men to learn lessons from abuse and injustice towards them.

In the Vedic and other ancient traditions, the masculine and feminine principles have been considered complimentary halves of duality, Shiv and Shakti, or Yin and Yang. The divine feminine is not related to gender or genitals, it is the feminine qualities of creativity, patience, forbearance, nurturing, motherly love, inner strength, spiritual power, surrender and sacrifice. The masculine is that of logic, intellect, decision making, being objective, outer strength, power and authority. Similar to the left brain. A man can have feminine qualities dominant, and vice-versa. Some people have an equal balance of both. In this very masculine world, there has been little appreciation for her inner power and qualities.

Now nature is bringing back the balance by raising the feminine Shakti principle. The Earth is being viewed as Mother Gaia. We are moving from the ego framework of service to self, to heart virtues like service to others. You see women in movies being given the role of the protagonist, and not just being used for their bodies. We see women's opinions are being given more respect in society, and their voices are heard. There is growing acceptance of women breaking free from control and dominance by male members of their family to choose what they want to do in life, get educated, and have a career if they like. It is no longer the case that women have to live in a shadow, though in some places on earth they are still treated worse than animals. With the balance of male-female coming back to earth, relationships are becoming supportive and true partnership, like two parts of a soul.

Soul Mates and Twin Flames

In our times so much is said about soul mates and twin flames. As creation happened, souls were created from consciousness, and consciousness descended from the highest most subtle realm (dimension/*Lokh*) to the grossest (physical). Therefore, as you go higher in dimensions, you will find a collective soul, or being. These higher souls often incarnate into lower dimensions as masters or avatars, and to interact with us they take on a personal form. Like a family tree, the one original soul at the highest dimension (*Lokh*) divided and descended down through the dimensions, much like cell division in a fetus. As cells belong to a particular organ, so do souls belong to soul groups. I've heard another master say that a collective soul divided seven times, first dividing into one male and one female, and then male into males, and female into females. Sal Rachele, an intuitive and teacher whom I learn from, says that souls were created in groups of twelve at each level of division. So each one of us belongs to a group of twelve souls, with a parent soul, which again is part of a group of twelve souls, which has a parent, and so on. Therefore, your soul belongs to a lineage of a soul family.

Within this soul group, there are couples, some call them soul mates, others twin flames. Now soul mates should not be confused with those with whom you have had a romantic relationship or marriage because those can be Karmic and they would only be for the purpose of settling accounts.

In a soul mate relationship, things are calm, complementary and steady. It is not infatuation or based on need. It is not driven by lust or longing for love. However; it is a deep connection and unsaid understanding. Both support each other in their life purpose, respect one another, and give each other space to be what they are. There is complete acceptance of each other as they are, no expectations, no demands. They are truly their other half, allowing each other to be and express who they are.

Life flows through self-expression. Without self-expression life lacks fulfillment and joy.

People may not like you for your self-expression. They don't accept you as you are. Why should you get affected? Everyone has their baggage. Let them deal with it. Why should you transfer their baggage to yourself? Let yourself remain free.

Extreme Pain brings Extreme Transformation

We shun pain and problems, we want to get rid of discomfort quickly, we sweep things under the carpet and cover up our troubles with a happy front. The normal way to handle problems in society today is to forget and get over them as fast as possible and get busy with life. This is the wrong approach. Pain is an opportunity to get over problems authentically. Avoiding pain makes it go into our subconscious mind, which makes it last much longer. Then it keeps surfacing from time to time, and unless we deal with it in this life it will re-surface in the next life with a similar situation, pattern and even the same characters.

Several ancient texts start with grief and misery. The Yoga Vasistha starts with Sri Ram in depression. The Bhagavad Gita starts with Arjun in grief. This is the starting point of a deep quest; the deeper the pain the greater the gain. Knowledge, revelation and realization then follow. A lot of saints including Meera Bai suffered great pain, which made their devotion single-pointed, and their surrender total; this pinnacle of Bhakti brought enlightenment.

Rumi said, "The wound is the place where the Light enters you."

Often pain is a blessing in disguise. Therefore, we need to go through pain, rather than suppress it into the subconscious or bottle it up. We need to feel, and go through the dark tunnel of discomfort, only then will life find full expression when it comes out into the light on the other end.

Go deep into the pain. When we go deeper and deeper into the pain with conscious awareness we reach the bottom point. That deep hole is the doorway to the other side. This requires witnessing and wisdom rather than drowning in the darkness of depression. It's a yogic practice. It is like a clogged pipe of emotion and thoughts, it doesn't let life flow. We need to move through it with self-effort, guided by wisdom and love. Work on it. That's the only way to get rid of it forever, else it is like postponing the lesson to be learned. If we don't pass a class we need to keep repeating it till we do. There's no other way. Pain and tragedy are opportunities for expansion of consciousness and growth of character. Once you cleanse yourself of the pain and mental turbulence you will see a beautiful smile emerge that will be unshakable by anyone or any event. Now you have become a stronger person from within. Only then can dispassion and detachment arise. The chains of the pains will drop and dissolve. The person who gave you grief will no longer be judged and disliked by you – they won't matter. In fact, you will have compassion for their ignorance, and even pray that they stop harming themselves and others because of their ignorance.

Seek to regain that unconditional love that you are! And remember that which you have long forgotten. Beyond the wavering love, with cycles of attachment and aversion, like and dislike, ups and downs, of the limited emotional love of duality...there is a field of love, of oneness where all dualities merge...we must function from there.

First, you have to start from within - to love yourself unconditionally. After layers of negative inputs that has pained and buried the heart, you have forgotten the feel of self-love. Others' harsh words create thoughts that cast shadows of darkness and pain, blocking out the light of consciousness. The heart has to somehow heal and re-emerge. The alchemist has to convert the shadow into light, poison into nectar, and pain back to consciousness. May the negativity burn in the fire of the *Yagya* of purification.

You have to love yourself, embracing all your shortcomings; how else will you love others with their imperfections? You have to love yourself as God loves you, and love others as God loves them. As my dear friend Nirmal said, constant affirmations of 'I love and honor myself' are needed.

You have been given a verdict of innocence. Let your guilt be flipped over years of blame, and so you are freed! Now is the time to dismiss and dispel that pain as a myth created by false belief, and fill yourself with love and light. The more you love yourself the more that love is served unto others, till there is only light and love - only that field of oneness where we all merge!

This is unconditional love.

4

Cultivating Unconditional Love

> *"Unconditional love is our birthright, not judgment and*
> *condemnation, and there's nothing we need to do to earn it.*
> *This is simply who and what we are."* ~ *Anita Moorjani.*

"How can you achieve a state of love other than by loving?
Love seems to be the great unifying factor amongst
humanity. All of the spiritual ideals from all wisdom
traditions involve the concept of love. Love is what binds
us together. Love is based on unity. To love something is
to be part of it in some way. In love the means and the
end are one and the same. If we are healed in all ways, we
inevitably arrive at the state of love. There is no way to
achieve the state of love other than by loving. Love quickly
moves from the realm of the expressible to the realm of the
inexpressible. We soon run out of ideas and ways to express
it, yet avenues of expression abound. Love is the expression
of selflessness. The ego with its desires and petty concerns
is subordinated to something greater than itself. The search
for love is the end of all meaning. Our search would be dry
and our attainments hollow if we lack love. Love is our birth
place, our final refuge and reason for being. If we recognize
that compassion and love are our ultimate destination of
our search, the heart of the universe itself responds. Love

is transcendental. Because it is beyond human limits, love evokes miracles that respond to the call of love alone. You within your heart are the expression of divine love. In fact you are that divine love. *'Aham Prema'*, I am divine love." – Thomas Ashley-Farrand

For those who have not found love from others, have never found the love within. They have not loved themselves, sometimes not even knowing what it means to love oneself. This lack of self-love makes them hungry for love from others.

The way you treat yourself is the way you will let the world treat you. Patterns of experiences repeat themselves till we integrate the learning and grow from it. It can be a relationship with a parent, spouse, child, or friend. It can be long and sustained, or short and intense. Our inner shortcomings attract the same lessons, till an inner blossoming takes place, and the light shines within.

We get affected by people and situations. Perhaps in my case, I have developed a deep impression that I am not loved or accepted as I am. Judgments have led me to lose my own self-worth, self-acceptance, and connection with others. These impressions within cause my soul to manifest experiences in which another person doesn't love or respect me. The impression deepens and the cycle continues until I work earnestly on taking myself out of the cycle of misery.

I have gone through many repeated patterns of experiences to learn the lesson of my life; to have self-worth, self-love, to honor myself, to hold myself in divine esteem, to nurture and pamper the child within me that feels no one loves her but whom I need to love and embrace. I need to accept and love myself as I am. I need to feel that I am a beautiful divine being blessed by God's loving grace. I need to value myself as much as God does. Then I wouldn't be treated as worthless, disrespected or abused. I need to hold on to my power and not give it away to be manipulated.

The amount one respects and loves oneself is the amount others will. When we love ourselves we are not adversely affected by others. This is not an egoistic love, but a knowing that I am love. When the love and light dawn within it is a beautiful feeling.

Life has brought several experiences to me for me to learn that I am loved, that I am love, and to love unconditionally.

When I was hit with distress, I was struggling to find solace for the pangs of pain in my heart. When a close friend betrayed me, I felt used, insulted, and abused. I was treated like garbage, dumped. I had given and given to an ungrateful person. Bullied by the ego and arrogance, I was treated as worthless. The suffering was so much I went into a deep sadness. Tears flowed from a wounded heart while this person remained numb and silent. While I begged for a response, no response came, till I bled and bled into a lifeless state. I talked to several clairvoyants, looking for the truth. I needed answers that would resound with me. I needed to understand what's happening, find solutions, and know the future. Why did this happen to me when I did nothing wrong? What is the lesson in this for me?

I looked and looked everywhere for the right answers. I read, I heard, I talked, and I searched within. I prayed, I reflected and meditated. I begged a Guru and God to give me answers and have mercy on me! I looked up into the night sky with tears rolling down and from the depths of my soul I cried, "Oh Divine! Tell me why?!"

Then one last night a dear soul friend of mine, Nirmal, shared a YouTube video with me. This came after I had gone through the suffering and searching I needed to experience, then I was ripe and ready to be given the answer. As I watched the video, great evolutionary realizations came. It laid out word by word what I had gone through and explained it with such clarity that I now understood what it was. It told me why it had happened, and what I had to learn from it. This tumultuous friendship was a crash course packed into three fiery months with great intensity. I had to learn the lesson of my life; to have self-worth, to honor myself, to respect myself, to hold myself in divine esteem, as a divine being of light. To love the beautiful person I am. Then I wouldn't be treated as worthless and disrespected or abused. I needed to hold on to my power and not give it away to be manipulated.

Patterns of experiences repeat themselves till we integrate the learning and grow from it. The pattern of this relationship was a repeat of a previous relationship. And the one previous to that. In one of the previous, less intense, relationships it took me over twenty-five years of bad treatment to realize that I needed to accept and love myself as I am. And when I did not fully learn my lesson from that experience, I repeated the same pattern with another relationship. Hopefully, now the blossoming into the next level of evolution needs to be complete. It's a great beginning. An evolutionary event. The suffering lasted long, but the realization came in an instant.

Just observe the longing for love within, and fill that longing with self-love. Observe the person within who is looking for love, and love that person dearly with divine love. Caress and embrace the inner child with love. Respect and honor the beautiful divine soul that is within. See the light within. You are worth it!

I gave myself time. I brought attention to my heart and awareness to my subtlest feelings. I pampered and loved that child within me that had been looking for love for so long. Over many lives and years, my heart that gave and gave, but was betrayed and abused, had started to believe that I was a worthless creature that no one loved. I lost all self-respect and self-appreciation. Then I became a beggar. Now it is time to know my own divine nature. Now the answers have started coming in.

Another friend wrote, "Your job is to look after yourself. Shed a little light on yourself and give your needs as much focus and warmth and compassion as anyone else's. Love yourself—accept yourself—forgive yourself—and be good to yourself, because without you the rest of us are without a source of many wonderful things."

For you, love has been about the other person, how much you can give. The other person may be like you, a giver, *Sattvik*. Or, they may be expecting an equal return, give and take, *Rajasik*. Yet others may be very sweet on the surface but later you find out they are self-centered, these are the takers, *Tamasik*. "The best relationships are those in which both are givers." (Emma Seppala).

Why are you hurt? What in you is hurt? The cause of anger and hurt is your own desire and ego. Love seeks love in return. When you get anger in return it tastes like poison. The expectation of love in return brings the pain. Anger comes when love falls short or when you dislike something. We all want love, and that desire for compassionate love in return sometimes disappoints. The more you love a person, the more your heart becomes open and vulnerable. We all want love, yet we are not always ready to accept love as it comes. Interestingly, we can only express as much love as much as the other person reciprocates. If you express more, they may not be able to digest, or understand why. There can be love mismatch, in the type and quality of love. Finally, you will end up feeling disconnected.

Is our giving of love unconditional? Is it compassionate? Is it dispassionate? If you receive a slap in return for your love, would you be able to absorb it with compassion and dispassion?

If love is dispassionate it would give, and ignore the response of anger, without it getting absorbed as pain. It would keep you balanced and centered. Use your wisdom to understand first and then respond calmly, or you may remain quiet.

So analyze your desire for love, which is masked and camouflaged in your loving. The one, who has found that love is within, that "I *am* love", will never demand love from anyone else.

When someone is under the influence of alcohol, or upset, they may say harsh words that hurt you, but it's good that at least now you know what they think of you. There can be a difference between what they say or don't say and what they really feel within. On the other hand, some may be acerbic but be a gem of a person at heart. It makes you wonder, if the negative side is the real person, or is the positive side? Take both, accept the whole person - that is love. The ultimate truth is even beyond both. There is yet another final core, which is their *being*, which is the only truth. And truth is love.

Sometimes we make mistakes by saying harsh words when we are moving a hundred miles an hour. We can lose someone in a hurry. Slow down! Be conscious and aware. When we say sharp words and upset someone: a) we may not recognize it, and not be apologetic; or b) realize it, but still not be sorry, because the ego wants to quickly cover it up by finding fault in the other person and then saying they forgive them, or trivialize the words spoken, side step the topic altogether and then act normal. Interestingly they can then return to showing superficial love and sweetness. If the ego does this in self-defense, a momentous opportunity is missed to evolve. So it's better to face it bravely and reflect. You have the choice to learn the lesson now or postpone it, repeat the mistake and bear the misery.

Reconciliation comes when both are reflective and ask for genuine forgiveness, and work on their relationship.

Whether you have hurt someone or been hurt, take it as a great gift to grow in love. This is the chance given to me by the universe to learn and remove that shortcoming in me that brings misery. Go deeper; see from the higher plane of dispassion. Hold the experience in your hands with grace. What's the lesson in it for me, what is the universe bringing to me? You have to ask sincerely, and the answer comes. A final solution to your problem is then integrated into you. Thank the other person for being an instrument of the universe. The path of the soul is towards having unconditional love for all.

It is very different when it comes to the love of a mother for her child. The unconditional love of a mother is divine love. A lot of mothers would agree with me when I say that, a mother will always say what's good for the child even though the child may not like it. It is the same for a father. I speak from my perspective, as a mother. Often what is good for the child is hard to say, and the child doesn't want to hear it. If a son is developing a bad habit, a mother will tell him to change it, fearless of being disliked. Some parents are more skillful and expressive of their love and other parents sound stricter. Though the personality and method may differ the intention of the parent is the same. A parent can't see a child develop a personality that is not based on values, or do things which are unbeneficial, unhealthy, immoral, illegal, or harmful. Some mothers and fathers are exceptionally good in parenting; knowing how to correct, how much to correct, what to correct, what not to get affected by. They give the child more space, respect, and are more loving in the way they tell a child to follow something. I know such mothers and have great respect for them. Some parents see black and white, micromanage, or do what might be called "controlling". They are more serious and strict, they correct too often, too much, and just need to let go. These parents may not be perfect or popular, however; the love is immense. Often the child doesn't understand that the mother wants what's best for the child, as opposed to another parent who doesn't say anything, but allows things that are not good for the child because they want to be liked by their child. The child often may think that a lenient parent is more loving, whereas it's just a difference in personality and expression, but the intention is always good and selfless. Saying yes to the child or not saying anything isn't a measure of love, in fact, it may be the opposite, where there's a bit of selfishness and a don't care attitude. When one parent is lenient and the other is strict, the children confide in the former and asks for permission from the parent who will say 'yes'. There is nothing in this world that can compare with the love a mother has for her child; it is absolutely unconditional. We all can have unconditional love, whether we have children or not; it needs to be taken for granted and then expanded it to everyone and everything. We must also take it for granted that we have love for the divine; never doubt it.

True worship or *bhakti* is to make the love we have for God universal.

May I love all as I love Him. May I love everyone as He loves them. May I see that oneness of the divine light in all eyes. May I become that Oneness.

How long and how much can you love an external God and dwell in duality? It then becomes idol worship and superficial. When we go deeper into the devotion we feel within for the divine, we start merging into our own inner experience of love, devotion, and bliss. That is our own consciousness, our Atman. We discover the divine within. The only devotion that lasts and reaches home is one that discovers that the divine is our own consciousness. Krishn is my own consciousness. Christ is my own consciousness. Then who do I worship?

That's not all. We then realize that our individual consciousness is the same as the universal consciousness; that all of creation is full of and permeated by a living consciousness. That feeling of one big whole that is beaming with love, that is alive and intelligent and that is all there is!

At the climax of loving, you become Love. At the pinnacle of devotion, you become the Beloved.

> *"A human being is part of a whole, called by us the 'Universe' —a part limited in time and space. He experiences himself, his thoughts, and feelings, as something separated from the rest—a kind of optical delusion of his consciousness. This delusion is a kind of prison for us, restricting us to our personal desires and to affection for a few persons nearest us. Our task must be to free ourselves from this prison by widening our circles of compassion to embrace all living creatures and the whole of nature in its beauty." - Albert Einstein*

Swami Vivekananda, a great saint of the 20th century, wrote an article on love which I really like:

"I once had a friend who grew to be very close to me. Once when we were sitting at the edge of a swimming pool, she filled the palm of her hand with some water and held it before me, and said this: 'You see this water carefully contained on my hand? It symbolizes Love.' This was how I saw it: As long as you keep your hand caringly open and allow it to remain there, it will always be there. However, if you attempt to close your fingers round it and try to possess it, it will spill through the first cracks it finds. This is the greatest mistake that people do when they meet love...they try to possess it, they demand, they expect... and just like the water spilling out of your hand, love will retract from you. For love is meant to be free, you cannot change its nature. If there are people you love, allow them to be free beings.

1. Give and don't expect.
2. Advise, but don't order.
3. Ask, but never demand.

It might sound simple, but it is a lesson that may take a lifetime to truly practice. It is the secret to true love. To truly practice it, you must sincerely feel no expectations from those who you love, and yet an unconditional caring."

Similarly, I have had a close friend whom I loved and lost because I could not learn the lesson of unconditional love. The lesson I have come to learn in this life is to give and receive unconditional love. The universe poses and bestows upon us such situations that are conducive for us to learn these lessons and that unfold into unconditional love. Another opportunity to learn these lessons will be crafted by the universe for me. This time, I will approach with awareness.

What is it that I'm experiencing?

It is exactly as has been said above but now it's time to live it.

I'm learning the painful test of sacrificing my desire for love by giving love and not expecting any. Life seems dry and boring like a wasteland without love. An inexpressible yearning for love exists in every single person. We all want to be loved by someone, by everyone. We want to be loved unconditionally, without expectations, demands, and control.

Yet our own ego wants to possess the person we love. We become unaware that we want to control them so they stay within the boundaries of our love. Where love is dependent upon our expectations being met, love is conditional. Ego always wants to get, more and more and wants to be satisfied by the constant showering of loving praise and attention. We think getting is fulfillment, but it's a trap for disappointment if not gotten, and craving for more if received. The craving for love that we feel, the thirst so intense, makes us chase a mirage of love. It results in continuous chasing and makes us more thirsty and tired.

Aren't we always expecting some love from the one we love?

We love and then want to be loved. We give and want to receive, and in greater amount! The moment this doesn't happen we are heart broken, suffering deep pain, and tears. We think this is the normal course of love and longing. But it is not. The love and longing in unconditional love is always about the other, in human love it's always about "me". The problem is that we are galloping on the horses searching for love, running wild through the forest and getting lost and delusional. We don't know the consequences; we need to have the wisdom to know where this ends up.

Why do we suffer pain and hurt in love? It is because people mistake love for other strong emotions, such as lust, or attachment through fondness. This is a delusion, *moha, this is the ego. Love is not an emotion.* Initially, we may see only the positive and fall in love or become close friends. When the high expectations and hopes of the honeymoon phase of the relationship fail to materialize, and the 'negative' characteristics of the other person are perceived; we then slowly fall out of love or lose the friendship. But we need to accept the whole person, as they are, both negative and positive. It's easy to love a perfect God, but very hard to love imperfect humans. That unconditional acceptance is true love.

Emotional love isn't true love so it changes, and when it diminishes, there are all sorts of dramas and complications. We are looking for that unchanging, everlasting love. True love is your own Being, an independent state, free from any external support or need. Emotional love is weak, it is always greedy or begging for love, not knowing what great treasure lies hidden beneath. Unconditional love is the king of hearts; it knows what wealth one already possesses. Isn't there a better road? No one likes to love a weak person, but everyone gravitates towards one beaming of love. Yet we usually choose the course that weakens us in love.

The problem is that we lack awareness. The moment we gain awareness we save ourselves from drowning in pain. It requires great discipline of the heart to turn it towards the higher love, the love that expands and leads to eternal bliss. So this is the practice, *abhyaas*, moment to moment putting your attention on every emotion, and questioning it. In short, it is a means to see how it is that we create the situations and circumstances that we find emotionally challenging. Armed with that knowledge, we can work on our consciousness, and discover ways through this maze into a more peaceful and enjoyable outcome. Instead of depending on others' love, fill yourself with your own love; there is plenty of it, that inexpressible feeling of sweet bliss within. It is there. If I let those emotions take hold then it leads to delusion and self-destruction.

You see that's why human love becomes bondage and when that same love is transformed to unconditional love, it sets you free. The transformation comes from cultivating unconditional love. We start off being able to love the things that we are culturally conditioned to love: the God of their religion, their family, and people who shared our world view. In order to emulate our Divine parents, and as we shall see, to free ourselves from many negative kinds of interactions, it is prudent for us to cultivate love in a growing number of situations and circumstances. Each one has embarked and needs to successfully complete an epic, heroic journey that culminates in our ability to love everything in creation. The great spiritual masters who have inspired humanity have in common their uncanny ability to love. Love issues forth from them in such a torrent that often the mind is rendered incapable of thought in the presence of such great souls. I have had the experience of utter stillness, reverence, unbounded love and awe in the presence of several great Gurus in my life. Not only do they love all the nice things that 'normal people' love, but Spiritual Masters love the not so nice people, circumstances, beings and parts of creation that none of us could. They can love the unloveable.

Unconditional love is a sense of expansion, selfishness a contraction.

Love is our nature, our default state, that's why we long for it because we have forgotten. Yet we sense it, we have felt it within, and it emanates from our soul, like a musk deer through a forest, following a scent that comes from within.

What we need is to maintain that awareness, that connection with the love within and be established in it. Then we will not look for love, but become an expression of it, all the time, in all circumstances, with all kinds of people. That would be an amazing state of being!

And that's what we long for. Isn't it?

What else is the purpose of life than to love everyone? Everything else fades in comparison. Nothing else is more important. If I can love everyone the way God loves them, the goal of this life would be reached. In our outer dealings, we have to be skillful, but we have to start from within, from a founding feeling of love.

Dispassionate Love

For those who are immersed in their true nature, are so fulfilled with the peace, love, and bliss of their own soul. Therefore; there is no need, desire, or expectation, nor are they affected by others' imperfections. This is true unconditional love, which is dispassionate.

There is a long road to dispassion. Often tragedies and broken relationships are a blessing in disguise, an opportunity to grow into unconditional love. The highest form of love is dispassionate compassion.

Often people misunderstand the meaning of 'dispassion'. Dispassion doesn't mean lack of love or loss of interest in practical life. Dispassion means being devoid of attachment and expectation. The love of true spiritual masters is also dispassionate, and they are the best example of dispassionate love. Their love and compassion are a natural expression, without effort, and it's their normal state at all times. Even being tough on a devotee/disciple, though it may seem harsh from the outside, is for their betterment and growth. If the devotee/disciple leaves, doesn't do anything in return, misunderstands the master, or hasn't developed faith yet, the master remains unperturbed. Like the sun, the love keeps shining unaffected and irrespective of our level of gratitude and awareness of its presence.

What is dispassion in love? It is love without emotion and feverishness. Love is not an emotion or a craving. Emotion belongs to the body and mind. Dispassion means devoid of desires. Unconditional love is dispassionate. With dispassion love doesn't waver or change, it doesn't depend on the other person or situation. It is unaffected by external influences. Like being in a warm and calm home while there is a storm outside, dispassionate love doesn't get affected by say, a person shouting insults, or the other person liking or disliking you.

How does it matter who's right or wrong!
Truth is Love.
Between right and wrong don't lose the love.
The mind divides,
The heart unites.
Love is more important than right or wrong.

Love is Truth.
Let love be Unconditional...

The Divine loves you without conditions! When you realize He is your own essence...you realize unconditional love's your own fragrance.

True love goes beyond emotions...it's being established in our own Being, which is love and naturally flowing to others.

We all long for infinite love,
Love purified is devotion – unconditional.
Then love is expansion,
There is longing in separation,
Wanting love is deception,
Then love is contraction.
Expectation and demand bring destruction,
Asking why and explanation destroys communication,
Heart to heart, soul to soul is the language of love.
When you want to merge with the other,
When there is only the other,
Love without emotion is devotion.
When there is "I" there is drama,
When is love unconditional?
When you love them just the way they are!
When you hug their perfection *and* imperfection,
Like the love of a mother.
When you love *in spite* of what they are,
Love is in giving, when love is without reason.
We are all looking for that divine love,
Looking for a soul mate to experience it,
Like a musk deer, we run from relationship to relationship,
Looking for that perfect love, the one that never dies,
which is as vast as the sky.
Looking for that pure love, the one that
time and events cannot touch,
With the manure of wisdom that matures
into ancient love over lifetimes!

That which is within you - the inexpressible!
Only the tamed turn in and find the soul as their mate.
Love for Krishn is elation.
Love starts with duality, a play of devotion,
Love completes in merging into Oneness.
Divine love *is* me! Is what I am made up of! It
is existence! Love is all there is! Love makes
the world turn, the universe vibrate!
It is the sound, Om! Love is bliss!!
Oh! My beloved! I long for that love!

Jesus – the Epitome of Unconditional Love

Yeshua (Jesus) is the most gentle, luminous, loving, kind and benevolent being. He serves us with his immense unconditional love. His love heals, and in the presence of His perfect purity of love there is instant healing. His love is unending, constant, and unwavering. He cannot but love us, He says. His love is so kind, He always wants us to see our inner beauty, and not have us identify with our vices. If we have guilt, shame or self-blame He first embraces us so lovingly, and then with kind and gentle wisdom he leads us step by step to discover our divine nature. He makes us feel so loved, and assures us that we are always loved, without fail, and even if we falter, He is there to embrace us, cradle us like children. His love for us restores the love present in us, the love that we are. He is a mirror of our soul and of our true divine nature. In His presence one starts resonating with the same divine love and light that he projects. He is a true role model for us to share our love with others; to serve, to heal, and to be a being of unconditional love. We are divine beings, created in the image of God, in the likeness of our creator. This is the truth of who we are.

Lakshmi – the anthropomorphized principle of Unconditional Love

Who is Lakshmi? I once asked. The answer was an experience of immense universal love enveloping me. That unconditional love is also very personal for me. Because humans can interact with a personal embodiment of that universal love, we have Lakshmi - with whom I feel a deep heart connection. She is personified as a divine mother who always provides because she loves. As I look around now I see everything provided to me in abundance because of that divine love. And she also comes to me through others; my mother, my friends, all those who provide so much to me because of that same love. *Lakshmi taam padmini-mim sharanam-aham pra-padhye!*

Sri Lakshmi is the abundance of love, the unending ocean of unconditional love. Personal love is a need. Limited. All of us have a need to be loved. There is feeling of lack. We keep seeking love like chasing a mirage and end up very thirsty. When wisdom overpowers the need the vast realm of love opens up. There is nothing but love. After many flip flops some get established in it. When we realize that we are always loved, and that we are also a reservoir of love, then there is no lack of love, no need to find love. Therefore; we no longer attract relationships based on need, rather we attract a person who resonates with us. Then the relationship is based on sharing love and supporting each other.

5

Anjali – A divine offering

S o how does one cultivate virtues such as unconditional love, humility, and so on? These virtues are inherent in our consciousness, and the impurities, vices, and muck needs to be removed to let the virtues shine through.

Praising others kindles the virtues in us, while criticism evokes negativity. When we praise, those divine qualities that we are praising illuminate within us (*Dev*). Notice how we feel inside, in our inner environment, when we praise and when we criticize.

Say, "You are so sweet, so loving, so beautiful...." and feel those qualities sprout within you. Praising itself is a divine quality.

We can only recognize divine qualities in others because they are present in us. We cannot recognize something that we can't identify with within. So often I say to a person praising me, this praise is a reflection of you!

When we criticize with emotion and intensity, "You have such a big ego! You are such an angry, hateful person!", then feel those same emotions burst within you.

The mechanics of praise and criticism is a brilliant design by the divine. You become what you praise. Praise and criticism reflect a truth about the person who is expressing it.

When someone criticizes you don't take it personally. It often reflects what they are, not you. However; you must use a wisdom filter to objectively siphon what criticism you can take constructively. On the flip side, don't let praise go to your head; know that those qualities belong to the divine, not something that your ego owns. The biggest virtue is humility. Therefore, offer all the praise that comes to you to the divine.

Or perhaps you have low self-esteem, and know your dark side, the demons within, and are too hard on yourself. Don't some of us feel that way? But it should not be so. There is a time to face the inner demons and vanquish them, and there is a time to accept praise. Sometimes it's very hard for us to take praise. That is also a subtle form of ego. Let us be simple and natural like a child. Always accept yourself as you are, embrace with love those uncomfortable feelings that come up. The degree to which you have loved and accepted yourself as you are, to that degree will you be unshaken by praise and criticism.

When we praise people, nature, God, those divine qualities come alive in us. So we should praise daily. That's why we have the rituals of prayer. Prayers, *pujas*, rituals, are meant to purify us. It creates a sacred environment within and without.

Let people praise you; know that it is good for them, because it is kindling those qualities in them. So recognize those qualities in them. Praise or be praised!

Why are half of our world's scriptures full of praise for the divine? Not just praise but beautiful, poetic, prayerful praise; as a divine offering - *Anjali*. I feel that half the Veds are full of divine songs of praise:

Devi Suktam, Sri Suktam, Narayana Suktam, Purusha Suktam (my favorite), and so on.

> *"vedAhametam puruSHam mahAntam | AdityavarNam tamasastu pAre | sarvANi roopANi vicitya dheera: | nAmAni krtvAbhivadan yadAste ||"* (Purusha Suktam v16)

Translation: This great Purusha, brilliant as the sun, which is beyond all darkness, I know him in my heart. Who knows the Purusha thus, attains immortality in this very birth. I know of no other way to salvation.

Vinita Dubey

From the various *Suktams, Stotrams, Panchakams, Shatakams, Ashtakams,* to *Stutis* galore, the Lord has been praised.

© *Credits*: Anjali Kalia, Divine Design, Noida, India

"Iśvarah paramah krsnah, sac-cid-ānanda-vigrahah
anādir ādir govindah, sarva-kārana-kāranam.
Govindam ādi-puruşaṁ tam ahaṁ bhajāmi" (Brahma Samhita 5.1)

Translation: Krishn, who is known as Govinda, is the Supreme Personality of Godhead. He has an eternal blissful spiritual body. He is the origin of all. He has no other origin and He is the prime cause of all causes. I worship Govinda, the primeval cosmic Being.

Brahma sang this *Stuti* to Narayan at the beginning of creation, after emerging from His navel. This is one of my favorite Stutis.

Then there are the Lalita Sahasranama (1008 names), Vishnu Sahasranamas - full of brilliant praise, devotion, prayer, offered to the Lord as an Anjali.

Gratitude is one of the most transformational and powerful feelings. Negativity is when there is fear, worry, pessimism, anger, hatred, greed, jealousy, arrogance, ego, and a host of other negative attitudes. It does not work to tell someone not to worry. To change a detrimental trait it's important to enhance a positive one. Like the saying, 'It's better to light a candle, rather than curse the darkness,' be grateful for what you have been given, and count your blessings. No matter what your situation, even if you are being tortured by an enemy, you can turn it around and see it from a perspective of gratitude. Even at the moment of death, you can be grateful for the good things you have had in life. Develop a habit to be grateful every day. You will see how your life will change around. Grace is directly proportional to gratitude. The more grateful you are the more grace will flow to you. When you focus on lack, the more you will manifest your thoughts. It is very difficult to change negative tendencies. That is why spiritual traditions have focused on transforming these tendencies to positive ones through spiritual practices, which include singing and chanting in gratitude to the divine.

Singing, Chanting, Sound, Vibrations

Singing sacred songs, and chanting have a very deep and profound effect on our system. In my study and research of sound and vibrations, I entered into a whole new realm of secrets about vibrations. Sacred chants like the Vedic Mantras, or Gregorian chants, are in the rhythm of the underlying vibrations of our existence. In my Shaman's words, "Empower yourself through the use of your voice. Using the sacred sounds you're going to entrain your physical body, every cell of your being to these sacred chants, which elevates consciousness. When you entrain to these sounds then you become the instrument, your vibrations resonate throughout your body, and elevates consciousness and can heal the physical body. That's why sacred chanting is done, because then you are the vessel, for those sacred sounds. That's what the words atonement and attunement have to do with sacred sound. To atone for one's sins, is really to break free of remnant vibrations that you have been living in, that's labeled as a sin, and all it is a frequency state. Once you atone and let go of that, you're bringing yourself back into an attunement with God, and you are resonating differently. And once you become a vessel and use your voice you are now vibrating, not only every cell of your being, but you're also bringing your brain into a different brain wave frequency. The EEG goes from Beta to Alpha to Theta. The slower the brain operates the more we have access to it. And those are the expanded states of consciousness and awareness. The slower the brain operates the more capacity it has, so when it slows down to between 8 – 12 Hz (cycles) per second that's Alpha state, above 12 Hz is Beta, which is our normal state of operating, up to about 30 Hz. So if you drop below this you go into meditative states and even lower into [Theta and Delta] expanded states of consciousness."

'If you want to find the secrets of the universe, think in terms of energy, frequency, and vibration.' - Nikola Tesla

There are many hidden truths to vibrations, these secrets were encoded in the Vedas. Each chakra has a vibrational frequency related to it. Let's look at the heart chakra, called Anāhata, meaning unstruck [sound]. Sound vibrations in the ether come first in creation. यं, Yaṁ, is for the heart chakra, and also the Beej (seed) mantra for meditation. It is a subtle sound like a thought, so said within, not spoken. The (gross) sound that can be pronounced for the heart chakra is 'haah'. Frequency is the key. Frequency of the heart is 528hz (the middle note in music, the middle chakra). After sound comes air, prana. The green blade of grass converts the energy from the sun, creates oxygen. After air comes light, in the light spectrum heart is green. Sound creates form, from matter and energy. This is demonstrated by Cymatics, that's the *Yantra*, sacred geometry. Geometry is about numbers and numbers are the language of creation. Water is liquid crystal. Our body is eighty percent liquid - crystal. When a frequency of 528hz is mirrored in the water it creates geometric patterns, *Yantra*, of the heart, the star of David, the two triangles. Therefore; each sacred geometric pattern, *Yantra*, has corresponding mantras at subtler levels. Because from vibration comes matter.

Heart is love when at 528hz, reverse is fear and hate. The emotion of love is a very large electromagnetic field of vibratory pattern. Our chakras are at the endocrine glands. Hormones are electromagnetically charged. Sound heals the soul. Love is the universal healer. Water is the universal solvent. Music is the universal language. As is the microcosm, the spiritual body of chakras, is of our collective consciousness, and so is creation or macrocosm, the seven *Lokhs*. There's much more that I'm still unraveling.

The sacred sounds and songs that have originated from the deep transcendental state of the creator, when sung, generate the same state in the one who sings them. These are set in the rhythm of the natural meditative breath. The rhythm of sacred sounds takes one into deep meditation and higher states of consciousness. The songs support this experience. I was told by more than one clairvoyant that my role and gift is to help people experience consciousness through meditation on these sacred sounds.

In the Vedic system of sound, *Nada Yoga*, each vowel sound, and musical note is associated with a chakra. These vowel sounds are found in most ancient mystical traditions including the Egyptians, (Jewish) Kabbala, Mayans, Native Americans, Tibetans, and so on. When the vowel sound is pronounced, such as 'Aa' one will feel the vibration in the associated chakra; for 'Aa' it's the heart chakra. I learned Sound Healing from Jonathan Goldman who is one of the best in the world and he has developed an extensive model of sounds and harmonics. The other person I discovered was an American Vedic *Drupad* singer, Shanti Shivani. She is an awesome divine instrument for *Drupad, Nada Yoga,* and sound healing. Talk about attunement with the teacher, each cell was strung with her voice. They say you resonate with the attainment of the teacher/master. The ancient Vedic system of sounds, combined by a pure, evolved and authentic practitioner can transform the entire being.

The tonal framework of the Vedas is set in rhythms called 'Ragas' and they have emerged from consciousness at the start of creation. When sung accurately, each has a unique effect on a human being, as they are in the rhythm of the underlying vibrations of existence.

At the substratum of our existence is consciousness. From consciousness comes the primordial energy (Shakti), then vibrations, from vibrations - subtle divine light, from light - matter. As our body is matter and of this three-dimensional reality, this subtle light is part of our subtle higher dimensional existence. Higher vibrations are subtler and closer to consciousness, which is the subtlest. Ancient meditators tapped deep into their consciousness and experienced these lights, sounds, and vibrations. They then formed hymns and chants that would create the resonance of these vibrations within, because vibrations are the link to consciousness, and brings one closer to the experience of consciousness.

Sanskrit and Hebrew are energy based languages first then meaning based. What does that mean? Each sound vibration carries an energy signature that conducts a certain effect in the physical and subtle realms. Therefore Mantras are energy formulas. These vibrations are already in creation so Sanskrit sounds were picked up by ancient Seers, "Rishis". The sound also describes the "feel" e.g. when you say "Shanti" it brings peace and the sound describes the feel vs. say, "Krodh". Sanskrit has many other amazing aspects. Other ancient languages have similar characteristics. The vibrations of the chants being more important than the meaning, the Vedic practitioners place great emphasis on training students to practice the correct intonation, rhythm and meter.

In 1984-1985, Dr. Peter Garjajev, the Russian biophysicist, and his team of Russian linguists were studying DNA and the ways light and sound vibrations communicate with what is today termed as "junk" DNA.

Scientists have found only 10% of our DNA producing proteins, and could not figure out what the other 90% of our DNA does, therefore terming it as "junk". Well, nature doesn't create junk. Now new research is finding out the role of this DNA. The syntax and semantics of these genes are similar to the way human languages are designed, and this DNA responds to precisely focused vibrational patterns of human languages. You can converse with your body (i.e. your genetic material) via vibrations and waves that can heal ailments, fine tune your health, control body functions, etc. without the need of any physical intervention like surgery or medicinal drugs.

The experiments by Peter Garjajev and his colleagues, about the vibrational behavior of our DNA has proven that DNA responds to extremely focused light and sound vibrations at particular frequencies and hence can be instructed to perform tasks or exchange information accordingly. That is why the extremely precise vibrations from the chanting of Vedic mantras and the light from the fire ritual (*Yagya*), was performed. It was for creating health at the cellular DNA level. The secret is the connection of mantras with DNA and the Rishis knew this. Mantras purify. Mantras are another whole mystical subject. A purified one can use mantras as formulas.

In one of their experiments, the Russian scientists were able to beam the genetic patterns of salamander embryos onto frog embryos and thereby instructed the DNA of frog embryos to convert itself into salamander embryos. And it did! Without any physical intervention, or surgery, or drugs, not even touching –by just beaming genetic patterns the scientists were able to convert frog embryos into salamander embryos.

Their research has led to many groundbreaking and paradigm-shifting discoveries with one of them showing that DNA is able to absorb and emit vibrations that spiral along the double helix in sacred geometrical form. Literally, DNA creates magnetized wormholes in the time-space fabric. DNA acts as "tunnel connections" between entirely different areas in the universe through which information can be transmitted outside of space and time. The DNA attracts these bits of information and passes them on to our consciousness." The researchers found that with the presence of light (photons) at a certain vibration, DNA activation and thus evolution can occur. It is this DNA activation that takes us to the next level of evolution.

Vibrations, therefore, affect our evolution and carry it to the next level of physical and spiritual ascension through DNA activation.

From vibrations came matter. The effect of vibrations on matter can be seen through the experiments of Cymatics. In this process, vibrations of different frequencies are passed through particles, or liquid, which forms perfect symmetrical patterns. The patterns change as the frequency changes. The symmetry and geometric forms that we see in nature have therefore been formed from the subtle vibrations as the basis. What is interesting is that the geometric shapes formed by different frequencies are very similar to the *Yantras*, or sacred geometry, of the Vedic and other ancient traditions. The vibrations from singing and chanting also create these patterns in our cells that are mostly water, bringing harmony. Sounds at a particular frequency, e.g. "Om", would have the same effect on cells that are not tuned well, as dropping a pebble on a disturbed surface of the water, which would then brings harmonious ripples.

Each object has a resonant frequency. Every organ, each human being has their own unique soul signature, so does each planet, and so on. When your soul, in the presence of an evolved being, your soul starts resonating with theirs, and you experience vibrational elevation it is like two tuning forks; when one is struck the other starts resonating at the same frequency. Each object a person wears for a while carries their vibrations. The places where spiritual practices or events happen carry a higher vibration in their subtle space. In locations where a person or persons have attained liberation, the transcendental vibrations stay for ages. Such become the places of pilgrimage. If you have become aware of your own subtle body you can feel these subtle vibrations from other people and places. In Bharat (India) there are many places which are pregnant with these sweet, divine, transcendental vibrations. For this reason, I love to visit holy places. I managed to go to on one such special place during my trip to Bharat.

6

The Epicenter of Devotion

‎---

A dios fatherland! I am going to my motherland - Bharat[5] - the land of the Vedas, where every particle vibrates with the Tapa and Moksha of the Rishis[6] over thousands of years. I am going to my birth town Kanpur, on the banks of the Ganges. I am going to celebrate my birthday in the arms of my mother. I am going to celebrate the birth of creation, *Navratri*, the nights to revere the divine mother with my mother divine.

Bharat - that ancient land which has a subtle soft essence that attracts each visitor not knowing what it is that pulls them back to this land again and again. It is the heart of the people to whom gentleness, hospitality and family feeling, *Apnapan*, makes one addicted to this place. Like wine is to France, machinery to Germany, spirituality is to India. There are more spiritual personalities, Pandits, Swamis, Babas, Rishis, per square mile in India than in any other country in the world.

I reach Bharat and feel so lucky that I can sit on the banks of the Ganges in Kanpur and meditate. Under me are layers and layers of an ancient civilization where so many have attained Samadhi. The vibrations still present in the subtle realm have purified the environment to make my meditation so deep and effortless; I simply have to close my eyes.

I wanted to go to Rishikesh on this visit to India, but it was too far from Kanpur for Mummy to be able to make that journey. I had looked at the map for any other spiritual/religious places in a radius of 2-4 hours from

---

5   Bharat – Known in the west as India.

6   Rishis – "Seers". Realized beings.

Kanpur. There's no shortage of historical religious places in India! My eyes fell upon Mathura-Vrindavan where I also wanted to go because of its association with Krishn.

Our initial plan was to go around Dussera, the tenth day after Navratri. However; due to some obstacles and inability to find accommodation we postponed it to the following week. Even that wasn't working out for some reason. We were going to go with my nephew, Gaurav, and his maternal grandfather, Nanaji. So the dates kept shifting and then finally Gaurav decided the dates. We would leave on Sunday for three nights. It was then that I found out that Monday was Sharad Purnima. Sharad Purnima was the full moon night of the full blossoming of divine love; the night of Krishn's divine dance, Raas, with the Gopis of Vrindavan. Somehow He made sure I was there that night.

A little bit about Nanaji. My parents and I would attend his talks on Ramayan at Gaurav's family home which is almost next door to us in Kanpur. Though a householder, he has a tremendous amount of knowledge and experience in the spiritual realm. Now that he's retired from his job I suggested to him, jokingly, that he should become a 'Babaji'! It's great that I can learn so much from him, and have spiritual dialogues with him as a family member. He can answer a lot of my questions, be my spiritual/religious Wikipedia. He's a resource into the spiritual/religious network and now our spiritual guide on the Mathura-Vrindavan trip.

So we're off to Mathura-Vrindavan. I can't wait to be with my Krishn. Will I get a vision of Him? Will He give me *darshan*[7]?

दिल में दीया जलाई के चली में हरी के पास ।
मन में बांसुरी सुनाई के आए गोविन्द मेरे पास ।
प्रेम भाव भर आई है चली में गिरिधर के द्वार ।
आनंद कृपा भर भर के आए गोपाल मेरे पास ।
हरी में लीन हुई में मिल गए सागर में साथ ।

---

[7]   There are two types of *darshan*. 1. When the devotee receives a vision of the divine. 2. When a devotee views and pays homage to an idol of the divine.

Dil mein diya jalai ke, Chali mein hari ke paas.
Mann mein bansuri sunai ke, Aaye Govind mere paas.
Prem bhav bhar aai hai, Chali mein Giridhar ke dwar.
Anand kripa bhar bhar ke, Aaye Gopal mere paas.
Hari mein leen hui mein, Mil gaye saagar mein saath.

Translation:

With a lamp lit in my heart, I proceeded towards the Lord.
In my heart I heard his flute, as the Lord cames closer to me.
The ecstasy of divine Lord overflows as I come closer to the Lord.
The Lord's blessings shower me as the Lord comes nearer.
I merge into the divine Lord, we become one in the ocean of
consciousness.

With Mummy being so devoted to God, Gaurav also spiritually inclined, our journey to Mathura was full of interesting spiritual stories and conversations.

We arrive in Mathura around sunset. Our stay has been arranged by Gaurav's uncle who is a senior manager in the Mathura Refinery. We had made bookings at another guesthouse in Vrindavan near the Banke Bihari temple, but Gaurav and Nanaji suggested against it. So here we are at the Refinery colony. Very green, open and lots of peacocks. Looks like Vrindavan! Gaurav's uncle, Mr. Tiwari, comes outside to welcome us. We sit down in his modest living room. Indians are very warm hosts and everyone is family. He confirms that he was able to book two rooms in the company guesthouse so looks like it'll be here that we stay. Not exactly what I wanted, it would have been better if we stayed in Vrindavan. Anyway, things happen. Mr. Tiwari, being a local, started educating us on the places of interest, their timings, and suggested a schedule for us. I ask him about how long he has been in Mathura and found out that his family has been here for five generations!

Nanaji and Mr. Tiwari spoke about Swami Guru Sharananadiji Maharaj and his Karshni ashram in Mathura. He's a highly esteemed saint of present day and has a beautiful ashram in Gokul. Apparently Mr. Tiwari has close contacts there and can arrange for us to be given special treatment and be escorted around. So we decided to go there this evening itself and be back for dinner. On the way, Tiwariji – whom I address as "Bhaiya" (brother) – tells us that the land the ashram is on and all the surrounding area has belonged to his family.

We got special parking at the ashram, left our shoes in the car and walked onto the sand. This place is called "Raman Reti". Raman refers to divine play and Reti is sand, so Raman Reti is the sand where Sri Krishn engaged in his divine plays, and walked barefoot on this land during his childhood. It was already dark so it was hard to get a broad perspective of the ashram. First, we met with lots of indigenous cows in a pen. They looked so clean and healthy unlike the cows elsewhere. Then my eyes fell upon a beautifully carved temple, a Shiv temple I was told. There was another one next to it and then the main temple. We entered the hall of the main temple. There was a beautiful statue of Radha-Krishn. Bhaiya explained the other statues of the Guru lineage of Swami Sharanandaji. The hall was full of devotees and Sadhus (monks), but it wasn't crowded. The temple and the whole ashram seemed pristine. We were then escorted through the rest of the ashram. There were Kutirs (hermitages) for monks, as any monk can come to this ashram, get food and lodging for free. We proceeded to the back of the ashram where there was a humongous bathing pool for the devotees. Nanaji has stayed here for a nine-day retreat. He told us a story of how the founder of this lineage, a Khan from Pakistan, became a devotee of Krishn and then he came here. Even though departed, it seems he comes here to bathe in the middle of the night in his subtle body. One day a night guard saw a man around 2:00 am coming and bathing in the pool and was rather scandalized. Nanaji tells me that there three things which are considered sacred in this area and should be given reverence: Raman Reti; the river Yamuna; and Vrindavan, where Radha-Krishn danced the Raas. So Nanaji takes some sand from the ground and touches it to my forehead. Our short visit to this ashram came to a close; it was truly a treat.

Now Bhaiya says we will visit Nanda Baba's house in Gokul. Nanda Baba was Krishnji's foster father, and this house is where his own father, Vasudev, brought Krishnji the night Sri Krishn was born. Baal Krishn and His foster parents, Nanda Baba and Yashoda, lived in this house till Krishnji was five. Since this land had belonged to Bhaiya's family, he said that his nephew was in charge of the premises, and would keep it open till we arrived as it was getting late. I found it ironic that I was visiting this house at night and Krishnji was also born and brought to this house in the middle of the night. The house was within a fortress; we could see the walls from the road. Nanda Baba was the local landlord and chieftain.

We arrived at the premises and there were a large number of steps leading up. We helped Mummy climb up one step at a time. We walked through the compound and into the house. As I approached the house and started walking in, I felt overpowering vibrations of sacredness, a fragrance of loving bliss, it's like submerging in an ocean of divinity. My heart felt an immense expansion and I felt transformed into bliss. These divine vibrations are felt in all sacred places or at sacred times or around sacred souls. The house is built of rocks, and there are lots of beautifully carved ancient pillars in the hall. In the main hall is a temple of the baby Krishn, Nanda Lala, His older brother Balram, His foster mother Yashoda and Nanda Baba. There were just a few people in the temple and we got special darshan. Bhaiya and his nephew told us about this house and the carvings on the pillars. We circumambulated the hall around the pillars and just as I finished and came back to the front, the temple pundits started the Ārti[8], with bells, chimes, and singing. Divine timing! I sat down on my knees with flooded hands, closed my eyes and dissolved into the sacred presence of the place. There is a very ancient, sacred, silent feeling here that I sense. I wished I could sit here alone a little longer. I bowed down and got blessings.

We finished touring Nanda Baba's house and then Bhaiya said he would take us to a Shiv[9] temple. Shivji had come to see Nanda Lala after he was born. This temple is connected with that event. Bhaiya's nephew also came along riding his motorbike in front of our car. We drove through this ancient holy place of Krishn at night; there was a sanctity about it. On the way, Bhaiya showed us the Brahmaand Ghat, the river shore where Nanda Lala showed Yashoda His universal form. The temple was about to close and we arrived just in time. Mummy is a Shiv devotee so she was elated to be there. The two priests waited for us to finish our darshan with the divine.

---

[8]   Ārti – A religious ceremony to honor the divine, like in a catholic mass.

[9]   Shiv – A Hindu God.

After this superb welcome at Krishn's birth town, it was time to go back. I told Bhaiya that he must have been Krishn's relative, it just felt like that, with his family lineage being from Mathura and all this land belonging to his family. It felt like I was being hosted by one of Krishn's own family members, that they welcomed me, found a place for me to stay, and took me to all these places of Krishn. Things just happened that night; we just flowed with them, like a raft on a river. It was like Krishn's divine hand was behind it. We were all in bliss driving back to Bhaiya's home. Bhaiya's wife had graciously made some dinner for all of us, which we were happy to consume after a long day. Then we headed to our guesthouse for the night. In bed, I thought, "I'm in the land of Krishn. I can't believe I'm here where He lived; this is the divine place of Radha and Shyam. Will I see Him? Will He come?"

Guesthouses in India are very nice; you get lots of pampering, personalized care and they are usually very reasonable. This guesthouse was very well maintained, the food was good, and the service was excellent. Mummy got a break from house work!

We got bed tea early next morning, the morning of *Sharad Purnima*, and were ready to head to Mathura. We were going to visit the Dwarka-dheesh temple, Krishn's birthplace, and the rest depended on time. The afternoon we planned to spend in Vrindavan. Nanaji told me to keep my smartphone in the car else it can either be pick-pocketed or snatched by monkeys. Nanaji knew a priest, in Mathura-Vrindavan known as *Punda*, who lived near the temple. We first went along the river Yamuna's shore, through all the *ghats* (piers) where there were lots of small shrines, shops, morning worshippers, and small alleyways. Everyone greets each other with *'Radhe-Radhe'* here. Radha Rani rules here as this is the land of the Radha *Sampradaya* (tradition). We found the priest, Chaturvediji, in one such alleyway who would now be our escort at the Dwarka-dheesh temple. Dwarka-dheesh is one of the names of Krishn. Dwarka is the name of a city in Gujarat, which was the capital of Krishn's kingdom, and *dheesh* means king/ruler. Incidentally, my great-grandfather built a Dwarka-dheesh temple in our ancestral town of Makarand Nagar, Kannauj, so our family deity is Dwarka-dheesh.

As in a lot of temples, there is a series of steps that leads up to the temple. All the temples have timings for *darshan* when the door of the shrine is opened for the audience. We had planned to be there before the doors got shut. As I entered, I again felt that sacred feeling, those divine vibrations. There was a huge crowd waiting to take *darshan.* The inner temple (shrine and hall) was surrounded by an open veranda, within the outer walls of the temple. The shrine and hall were on a raised platform climbed by another series of steps. In the middle of the hall was a pair of railings with people on both sides leaning over to see the idol in the inner shrine. There's always a mad rush at these public places. It's very important to keep one's focus on the Lord and maintain that deep connection with Him within; otherwise you would get lost in the chaos and lose this chance to experience the bliss. Most people are single-mindedly cramming for their personal *darshan* with the Lord, unconscious of others around. Some with their eyes closed were reciting a prayer, unaware of the loud crowd. Nanaji helped me get through a pile of people and lean over the railing to see the idol of Dwarka-dheesh and Radha-rani. You usually get only a few seconds before being pushed out. The temple is beautiful, around five hundred years old. There are beautiful murals on the ceiling. I spent a little time being on my own around the temple, to get its sacred feeling. I then circumambulated the main hall and shrine as is customary in Vedic worship. It was just amazing to see the amounts of people that come here, day in and day out. I wish I could visit this temple without this crowd, like last night's temple; we were more concerned with the pushing and shoving than being in the presence of the divine. After the temple visit, I bought a few *puja* things from a shop outside the temple.

It was time to see the birthplace of Krishn. The roads were jam packed because of *Sharad Purnima.* Gaurav decided to enlist a *Punda,* against Nanaji's wishes, to be our guide. His name was Pandit Chaturvedi. A short fair person, I was very impressed by his clothes, clean, ironed, green striped *kurta* and white *dhoti.* Krishnji's parents, Devaki and Vasudev, were imprisoned by Devaki's demonic brother Kansa. So Krishnji was born in a prison cell. Several temples were built and then destroyed by the Muslim invaders of Bharat. Today the temple shares a common wall with a mosque. Due to the tense religious sentiments of Hindus and Muslims about this place, there is a lot of security here. The Pandit kept addressing me as

"Rani" (queen) rather than the usual "Behen" (sister). He was quite sweet and quite diligent about explaining everything. The temple was very nice and clean compared to the Dwarika-dheesh temple. As I gazed around I thought that somewhere far below the earth's surface lay buried the original birth place of Sri Krishn. Krishn walked this earth more than five thousand years ago, about the same time as the Indus Valley civilization. We were probably walking on top of the original city of Mathura and Vrindavan. No significant excavation or carbon dating has been done here, unlike Dwarka. Pandit Chaturvedi not only escorted us back to our car but also helped us find a car tire shop to get air as someone had deflated a tire while it was parked. Gaurav thanked the Pandit and gave him his modest fees. Just as we were about to push off, he came to my window and said to me personally (in Hindi), "When you drop the 'I', you will get the *darshan* of Krishn." I was quite taken aback with such a philosophical statement coming from an ordinary pundit. Then we left and I looked back at him walking away. I *was* longing for Krishn *darshan*, how did he know? And why was he addressing me as "Rani", did he know who I was? Who was he? I thought about what he said, that when you drop the "I"ness, the veil that separates me from the divine; then Krishn, who is already there, will be witnessed. Krishn is my *Atma,* my soul, my consciousness. My longing to see Krishn was to be achieved within. Krishn, the divine, is within. That morning during my meditation when I was longing to see Him, outside, nothing happened, but I felt something inside. As soon as I turned my attention inward I could feel a ball of luminous bliss. That was Him!

So we drove away from Krishnji's birthplace and in the early evening of *Sharad Purnima* we visited *Nidhi Van,* or *Nikunj,* the grove where the mystical dance with the divine, *Raas,* first took place on this very full moon night. It is considered the most sacred place in terms of divine love, the epicenter of devotion.

The *Raas Leela* of Krishn and the *Gopis*[10] symbolizes the eternal cosmic celebration of creation and consciousness, the dance of duality. Krishn is consciousness and the Gopis are creation. The hundred and eight *Gopis* represent all the elements of creation (*Tattva*). He is the caretaker of creation, Gopal, and holds all the elements together. The longing of the *Gopis,* the urge to merge with their beloved, was like the gravitational pull of a black hole. I knew, I felt it. The sun holds the rays (Gopis) together. They dance to His tune, the tune of the flute He plays. So also, the mind forever longs to merge back into the soul. I long to be with Krishn night and day, I beg Him to come; there is no power within my being stronger than this urge. And the Gopis...they were with Krishn when He walked this earth! Even the Devis and Devatas were here with Krishn to be with Narayan. Why? Because only in a human form can one experience the intoxication of devotion. Exponentially so was the devotional rapture of the Gopis who were with their beloved. The immense attraction between Krishn and the Gopis is *Ras* (the sweetest nectar) and when the mind is full to the brim, on this full moon night, it is *Raas Leela.* When Narayan danced here with the Gopis, it moved the entire cosmos to dance in rhythm. Such is the story of their divine play, *Leela.*

---

[10]   Gopis – known for their highest unconditional devotion for Krishn.

83

Krishn was an *Avatar* of *Narayan*, the perfect manifestation of the conscious life force in a human nervous system. To sustain human life and excel we need nourishment and prosperity. *Lakshmi*, the spiritual consort of *Narayan*, symbolizes this aspect. *Radha-rani* was the manifestation of *Lakshmi* and the consort of Krishn. In Vrindavan you will not find any idol of Krishn without Radha; whereever there is Krishn, there is Radha. Radha was actually older than Krishn. *Lakshmi* is older than *Narayan*! Krishn was around ten years old at the time of the *Raas Leela*.

Now this garden of love is an enclosed orchard of *Kadamba* trees. What is amazing is that the ground is dry and parched, yet the trees are full of healthy leaves. The grove is shrouded in mystery; no one is allowed to stay here after overnight. I was told that even the monkeys and birds here leave at night. It is believed that Radha, Krishn and the *Gopis* still play the *Raas* here every night. There are stories of people who dared to stay overnight who became dumb, blind or insane by the next morning because it's beyond human capacity to witness the proceedings of the night.

There's a rapture I felt on that spot in the groove where the *Raas* took place. For most of the visit I was with Mummy, Nanaji, and Gaurav, but I did take a few moments to be alone on the platform, *Rasa sthal*, where the Raas took place. There is a "magical force" there and I started walking in the steps of the Raas. It was enchanting and it captured my mind and I went into a trance like ecstasy. For a few moments I was completely my true natural self. Nanaji saw me and realized that I had gone into another state. I think he was a little afraid so he took me by the hand and brought me along with him.

A famous devotional saint, Swami Haridas, used to meditate here and sang to Sri Krishn. It was here that his devotion invoked the apparition of Krishn. Swami Haridas asked Krishn not to leave and forever give him *darshan* and so Krishnji granted an image of Himself, the famous idol of *Kunj Bihari* now called *Banke Bihariji*[11].

---

[11]   *Banke* means bent in three places, it's the pose in which Krishn stands. *Bihari* means supreme enjoyer.

Swami Haridas was a great devotee of Sri Krishn. He was also the Guru of Mian Tansen, the famous singer in the court of Emperor Akbar. Akbar came in disguise with Tansen to hear Swami Haridas sing here in Vrindavan. Swami Haridas sang to the Lord in ecstasy, in a transcendental state; it was so pure and overpowering that even Akbar was swept away in the tidal wave of divine love.

Initially, the idol of *Banke Bihari-ji*, or *Thakur-ji*, was in *Nidhivan*; now the idol is in a temple in Vrindavan, probably the most popular temple here. We went to visit this temple the next morning. There were beautiful flower stalls outside the temple, so colorful, fresh and fragrant. I love flowers. We got some to offer *Bihari-ji*. We were able to get a side entry into the temple and avoided the long lines because of Mummy's knee condition. Again, there were a lot of excited people, high decibels, chaos, pushing and shoving. I somehow managed to help Mummy climb up to the main shrine. A priest shouted to us to give him the offering we brought for *Bihari-ji*, which he would take inside, and then we would wait for him to bring it back after it was offered and blessed (*Prasād*). We got to see the idol from the closest point to the inner shrine for a few seconds.

After *darshan* I helped Mummy back out and found a place for her to sit. I told her that I would go back from the main entrance to receive *darshan* because I was not satisfied and I wanted to be alone. So I went back in and slowly paced forward with my eyes transfixed at *Banke Bihari-ji*. He seemed alive; a tremendous amount of energy seemed to emanate from the shrine. Luckily it wasn't too crowded and I could stand there and get my timeless moments of silence in union with the Lord. It's hard to take your attention off him and leave, but I felt the others were waiting so I headed out. I received special *Prasād* from a temple priest and at that moment, I felt like I had come back home to my father, Krishn, was being treated like family and being honored by Krishn through his priest. I felt so humbled and like a child. I then did *Pradakshina* (circumambulation) of the temple. We spent time sitting outside the temple before leaving.

Our trip to Mathura-Vrindavan was drawing to a close. I had learned and experienced so much during this trip. Nani-ji told me so many beautiful things about devotion on our drive back. There were endless stories about

Vinita Dubey

Radha, Krishn and the Gopis of Vrindavan that we were leaving behind. This land and the people here are forever soaked in the sweetness of devotion, in the dance of ecstasy, their hearts full of longing for the Lord.

मैतो प्रेम दरशन की प्यासी
क्यों कान्हा मोहे दर्शन दीजो नाही?
सबको दर्शन दियो प्रभु तुमने -
हरिदास को निधि कुञ्ज में
मीरा को यमुना तट पे
सूरदास को भी आधी रात में
मुझसे ही क्यों तुम मिलत नाही?
आई थी में तेरे कुञ्ज में बिहारी
प्राण से गोविन्द! गोविन्द! पुकारी
बस एक आड़ बीच में रह जाए
आएँगे एक दिन गिरिधारी
अभी तक सिर्फ झलक दिखलाइ
मन को साफ करुँगी में
दिल में फूल सजाऊँगी में
गोविन्द कैसे नहीं आएँगे फिर
इस बार जाने नहीं दूंगी में
बस ये तड़प सागर में मिल जाए
पूर्ण होए यह जीव प्राणी

Mae to prem darshan ki pyasi
Kyo Kanha mohe darshan dijo nahi?
Sabako darshan diyo prabhu tumne –
Haridas ko Nidhi kunj mein
Meera to Yamuna tatt pe
Surdas to bhi aadhi raat mein
Mujse hi kyu tum milata naahin?
Aae thi mein tere kunj mein Bihari
Praan se Govind! Govind! Lalakaari
Bus ek aadha beech mein reh jaae
Aaenge ek din Giridhari
Mann ko saaf karongi mae
Dil me phool sajaaongi mae
Govind kaise nahin aaenge phir

Is bhaar jaane nahin doongi mein
Bus ye tadhap saagar mein mil jaae
Purna hoe yeh jeev praani

Translation:

The thirst for His presence is so great
Why is it that He doesn't grant me His presence?
To others You have appeared and graced –
To Haridas in the forest of Nidhi kunj
To Meera on the banks of the Yamuna
To Surdas in the midst of the night
Why do You not come to me alone?
I came to visit the forest where you dwell Bihari
From the depths of my soul I cried, Govind! Govind!
Was on the brink but something remained as a veil
One day He shall have to come
I will purify my mind
Will blossom in my heart
How can He not come then
This time I will not let Him leave
May this yearning merge into the ocean
Then this individual soul will become whole into the One.

7

Gopis of Vrindavan

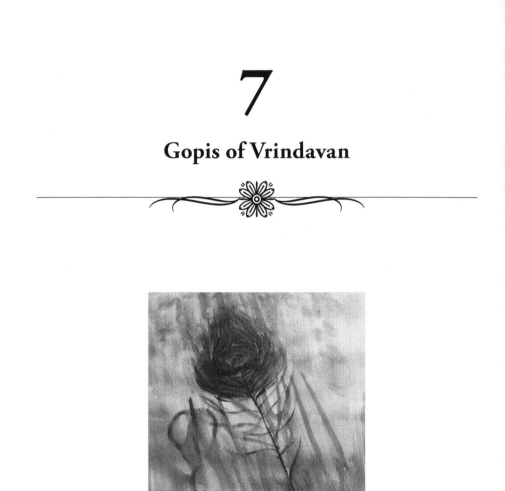

© Credits: Nisha Diddi

When I came back to the USA, I started listening to the magnum opus of devotion, "Srimad Bhagavatam" or "Bhagavad Puran." Bhagavad means, for Him and by Him, the Lord divine. This great text was written by the sage Ved Vyas. There are twelve volumes, cantos, to this text. The tenth canto is dedicated to Krishn. After listening to the introduction and a bit of the first canto I couldn't wait so I jumped to the tenth canto. As I heard the birth of Shri Krishn, the place where he was born, the house of Nanda Baba, it brought in the feeling and the fragrance of those places I had been. Now when I look at baby Krishn, the devotion has a different flavor, because I have tasted the devotion of Mathura-Vrindavan; it brings back those same feelings.

The heart of Bhagavatam is the story of Sri Krishn and the Gopis. Listening to the words of these Gopis one becomes immersed in the emotions of *Bhakti*.

Gopi: How can you blame me for being so absorbed in Govind, losing my mind to mundane things? I'm dancing drunk in the bliss of devotion. Singing, smiling, mind moving to the music, there's no room in my mind for any other thought. It is captured by the divine presence of Govind Damodara Madaveti.

*"vikretukAmA kila gopa-kanyA
murAri-pAdArpita-citta-vRittiH
dadhyAdikaM mohavashAd avocad
govinda dAmodara mAdhaveti"*[12]

Translation:

Daughters of Gops/Gopis deeply engrossed in the lotus feet of Govinda, while selling curd/butter in Braj, calls loudly the names of Govind, Damodar, Madhav instead of milk products. Such was the level of absorption.

A Gopi is one who drinks the love, beauty, splendor and divinity of Krishn through the senses and becomes drunk - drunk with divine love.

Neither Radha nor any of the Gopis' names are mentioned in the Srimad Bhagavatam. Why? Because only one who still has an ego has name and form. For one who has merged into the Lord, the identity, the boundary has dropped and has no name, no form. There are other reasons too. Srimad Bhagavatam doesn't mention the name of Radharani or the Gopis. There are elaborate descriptions of them in Brahma Vivarta Puran, Skanda Puran, Garga Samhita, and other Vaishnav texts.

---

[12] The Stuti (praise of the Lord), 'Govind Damodar Madhaveti', was composed by Sri Bilvamangala Thakur and has been sung by one of the greatest classical singers of all time, and my favorite, Pandit Jasraj. Not only is he a legend, but he's also a great devotee of the Lord which brings the sacred songs to life. When stutis are sung on Ragas by a great devotee and that too by such a musical maestro as Panditji - the resonance and effect within one becomes exponential. If the same stuti is sung in non-Raga form the rhythm and vibrations are not there.

There were eight main (Varistha) Gopis. Why eight main Gopis and wives? Eight is the number for Maya - creation. Maya is the Shakti (energy) that manifests. Gita Ch 7, *Ashtadha Prakriti* is eight-fold, the five elements, mind, intellect, and ego. Krishn is married to Maya, the ocean is wedded to all the waves. How many manifestations? Countless, even 16,000 is less.

Here is how Sri Satya Sai Baba explained eight main Gopis and wives, and 16,008 Gopis and wives:

"The *hridaya chakra* has eight petals. God is the Lord of the eight-petaled *hridaya chakra*. These eight petals are regarded as eight consorts of the Lord. In this context, the Lord is adored in the form of the Sun. The world cannot survive without the Sun. The solar system is derived from the Sun. Hence, the Sun is worshiped as Divine...

The ancient sages adored the eight-petaled divine center in the heart and thereby reached the sahasraara chakra and enjoyed supreme bliss.

The sahasraara chakra has a thousand petals. Each petal carries sixteen phases (*kalas*). Thus, the sahasraara chakra is said to represent 16,000 cowherd maidens (*Gopikas*) while the eight petals of the hridaya chakra are adored as the main consorts of Krishn.

The ancient sages reached the thousand petaled Sahasrara through the adoration of the Lord in the eight-petaled lotus of the heart. They used all their God-given intelligence for this spiritual goal. The sages considered the cultivation of virtues, good qualities, and righteous conduct as true education.

What do the eight petals of the heart represent? They are; love (*prema*), truth (*sathyam*), forbearance (*sahanam*), sacrifice (*thyaga*), compassion (*daya*), beauty (*sundaram*), bliss (*anandam*) and peace (*shanti*). To realize the bliss of the Divine, all the other qualities have to be fostered. God is the embodiment of all these eight attributes. Sacrifice is the most important of them." -- (Sathya Sai Baba Divine Discourse: "Promotion of Unity: Students' Duty" 14 Jan 1998. Prasanthi Nilayam).

These divine *Devis* of *Maya* (*Adi Shakti*) descended on earth along with Krishn when He took the form of avatar. Here are the Varistha Gopis:

1. Lalita Sakhi: Of the varistha gopis, Lalita is the most important, being the leader and controller. The beauty of all the other gopis appears to be conserved in the form of Lalita-devi. She is contrary and hot-tempered by nature. In an argument, her mouth becomes bent with ferocious anger and she expertly speaks the most outrageous and arrogant replies. When the arrogant gopis pick a quarrel with Krsna, she is at the forefront of the conflict. When Radha and Krsna meet, she audaciously remains standing a little away from them. Lalita was Radhika's best friend.

2. Vishakha Sakhi: Her attributes, activities and resolve are all much like those of her friend Lalita. She is an expert on all aspects of amorous diplomacy, and is the perfect counselor.

3. Campakalata Sakhi: She is an expert at the art of logical persuasion, she is a skilled diplomat, and she is a gourmet cook!

4. Citra Sakhi: Citra-devi is very talented. She is an expert in playing music on pots filled with varying degrees of water. She is learned in the literature, gardening, cooking, preparing beverages, and many other things.

5. Tungavidya Sakhi: She is a learned one. She is very devoted to her seva of dancing and singing, and is an expert at playing the veena. She is learned in rasa-shastra (transcendental mellows), is learned in the eighteen branches of knowledge, in niti-shastra (morality), dancing, drama, literature and all other arts and sciences. Being hot-tempered and expert at dissimulation, Tungavidya is one of the leaders of the gopis.

6. Indulekha Sakhi: She is contrary and hot-tempered by nature. She is learned in the science and mantras of the Naga-shastra, which describes various methods of charming snakes. She is also learned in the Samudraka-shastra, which describes the science of palmistry. She is an expert at stringing various kinds of wonderful necklaces, decorating the teeth with red substances, gemology and weaving various kinds of cloth.

7. Rangadevi Sakhi: Her personal qualities are much like those of Campakalata. She is always like a great ocean of coquettish words and gestures. She is very fond of joking with her friend Srimati Radharani in the presence of Lord Krishn. Among the six activities of diplomacy she is especially expert in the fourth: patiently waiting for the enemy to make the next move. She is an expert logician and because of previous austerities, she has attained a mantra by which she can attract Lord Krsna.

8. Sudevi Sakhi: She is the eighth of the varistha gopis. She is sweet and charming by nature. She is the sister of Rangadevi. Her form and other qualities are so similar to those of her sister Rangadevi that they are often mistaken for one another. She is expert in training male and female parrots and she is also an expert in the pastimes of roosters. She is an expert sailor and she is fully aware of the auspicious and inauspicious omens described in the Sakuna-shastra. She is expert at massaging the body with scented oils, she knows how to start fires and keep them burning and she knows which flowers blossom with the rising of the moon.

It was an autumn full moon night, *Sharad Purnima.* The warmth of the air mingled with the cool night, just right. Late into the night, the moon shone, in the silence, the ripples of the river Yamuna, moonlight shimmering. The toads croaked and crickets chirped. Then walked onto the green grass, light blue feet, with anklets, and the most graceful gait - there He was - Sri Krishn! with large, deep, seductive eyes, that take you into a trance, and a half smile, His face of transcendental peace. Then he lifted the flute to his lips and crossed his right leg over the left. As He started filling Prana into the flute, everything became alive. The notes flowed out of his flute, and nature felt silent to listen; the toads and crickets became quiet. A gentle wind came to greet Him, carrying the scent of the Kadamba flowers, filling the garden of love with divine incense. The flowers seemed to open as though in bliss, and branches danced to the rhythm of Murari's flute. As the notes of his flute carried to the Gopis' ears, they sensed the divine melody and as though in rapture, froze where they were. Following the flow of the music, they were drawn to Him, leaving their homes and fastened to the source. In the Kadamba garden of Nidhi kunj He was waiting for them, gleaming in the moonlight, in the dark night His blue skin with sparkling ornaments, and bright yellow silk *dhoti*. Seeing Him such, with that intoxicating flute, their minds were entranced, a most beautiful moment. The grove looked decorated with flowers and filled with sweet scent. He looked at them, smiled and then led them into a dance, the Raas Lila, the divine dance of duality, of consciousness with creation!

When the Maha Raas dance commenced between Krishn and the Gopis, the Gopis got this thought, "I" am special, Krishn loves me more than others. This is called 'Satvik Ahamkaar'. That very moment, Krishn disappeared. Why? The veil of separation, the ego came and consciousness was no longer visible. Darshan happens the moment the "I" drops, the veil drops, the boundary, the separation drops, and there is union. Consciousness merges with consciousness. Purna MeVaav Shishyate! Where ever there is a merger of creation and consciousness, there too this Maha Raas is happening, even today.

On the night of the Maha Raas, there was one Gopi who didn't get the Satvik Ahamkaar. When Krishn disappeared the Gopis looked for Him in despair. They saw His footprints with another pair of footprints, that of a Gopi! The Gopis were so jealous.

Who was she? Who was that Gopi who remained submerged in Krishn, who remained the most humble, innocent and childlike?

Radha is Bhagavan's *Hladini Shakti*, the delighting power is called Radha.

Krishn delights all the Gopis but she who delights Krishn and His devotees is Radha.

Only Radha delighted Krishn like no other.

Radha is like an adjective, a *Bhaav*, not a noun.

'Raadh' means to worship, she who worships the Lord. When our thoughts are turned towards God it's called Radha. The longing and the force merging into Krishn consciousness is Ra-dha. Dha-Ra is the opposite, flowing away from the source.

Maha Raas

After Krishnji disappeared, the Gopis, with great desire and wailing voice, in melodious tones and in several ways, wept out loudly. They couldn't stand the separation after the start of such an enchanting encounter with their Lord. They looked for him everywhere, called out to him, and sang out of pain. The most devotional poems come when there is the greatest longing from separation, *virah.*

> *"Jayathi thedhikam, janmana vruja,*
> *Srayatha indira, saswadathrahi,*
> *Dhayitha, drusyatham dikshuthavaka,*
> *Thwayi druthasavasthwam vichinwathe"*

Translation: Because of your birth in this Vrij this has become even more auspicious.

Even Indira, Lakshmi comes to live here because it's more glorious than *Vaikuntha.* We are yours, and we love you and we have to look for you everywhere. Our Pranas are in you and we are searching for you. Please come before us!

"Na khalu gopikaa nandano bhavan,
Akhila dehinam antharathma druk,
Vikhana sarthitho viswa gupthaye,
Sakha udeyivan sathwatham kule."

Translation: You are not the baby of Yashoda, Oh Krishn,

You are the soul of all beings, Oh Krishn,
By the request of Lord Brahma, Oh Krishn,
You have appeared in our clan, Oh Krishn,
To save the world, Oh Lord who is our friend.

Thus, they sang the *Gopika Geet*. When tired and almost dismayed, He re-appeared before them, wearing the yellow silk garment, several garlands, and with a smile on his face. He who is capable of making the God of love yearn for His love came back to the Gopis.

Someone came running and sat down on the grass next to him. One Gopi held her hands under her chin and just looked at him wonder- stuck. One started singing praises, one dancing, one put her head on his shoulders.

"aparanimishad-drigbhyam jushana tan-mukhambujam apitam api
natripyat santas tac-caranam yatha" (Srimad Bhagavatam 10.32.7)

Translation: Another gopi looked with unblinking eyes upon His lotus face, but even after deeply relishing its sweetness she did not feel satiated, just as mystic saints are never satiated when meditating upon the Lord's feet.

"tam kacin netra-randhrena hridi kritva nimilya ca pulakangy
upaguhyaste yogivananda-sampluta" (Srimad Bhagavatam 10.32.8)

Translation: One gopi took the Lord through the aperture of her eyes and placed Him within her heart. Then, with her eyes closed and her bodily hairs standing on end, she continuously embraced Him within. Thus immersed in transcendental ecstasy, she resembled a yogi meditating upon the Lord.

Surrounded such by these Gopis saturated with the sweet nectar of divine love, was Krishn. They wanted the fulfillment of their longing through the bliss of devotional singing and dancing with Him. Govind knew he had to quench their desire for the divine in accordance with their *bhav*.

Then the Maha Raas started, Sri Krishn danced with the Gopis, like the ocean dances with the waves. With Bhagavan Sri Krishn in the middle and Gopis dancing around him, was like thoughts revolving around consciousness. Then between each pair of Gopis was Krishn, dancing, like consciousness between two thoughts. And finally each Gopi danced with Krishn, the last thought dissolving into consciousness.

It was a merging of souls, Gopis with their Giridhari, the union of many into one; there was no body consciousness at all. That bliss in which all the levels of our existence are fulfilled - that's *Rasah*. That is *Brahmananda*. That infinite *Anand* - no words can reach it, the mind becomes silent, and no desires arise. The waves merged into the ocean and became One.

It is this merging of the individual into the infinite that is also the pinnacle of the path of knowledge, *Jnan*. That is why Sri Krishn sent his wise friend, Uddhav, who excelled in Vedanta, to meet the Gopis of Vrindavan. Sri Krishn wanted Uddhav to learn that the paths to liberation, Karm, practice, devotion and knowledge are intertwined. A fully ripe one-pointed devotion has the deepest wisdom. When Uddhav was lecturing the Gopis on Vedanta they seemed uninterested. One Gopi said, "With which mind do you want us to listen to you, Uddhav, the one mind that I have has gone and merged with my Krishn."

Bhakti in the Gita

It is this cocktail of Karm, Raj yoga (spiritual practices), Bhakti and Jnan that is also explained in the chapter on Bhakti in the Gita. Chapter twelve of the Gita is amazing because the first part of the chapter talks about devotion for the divine, and the second part talks about the virtues of a devotion that need the unconditional love for others. So both love for God and love for others is covered.

Bhakti is there in every soul and it evolves over time and births.

In the twelfth chapter of the Bhagavad Gita, Sri Krishn talks about a ladder of Bhakti. Here is the ladder of devotion from the first rung to the top most. The lowest rung of the ladder is when the tendencies and impurities in us are at 80 percent. At this stage starts the purification by doing everything as an offering to the divine, taking the fruits of actions as God's offering. "Fruits of actions" is a technical term that means, "drop the worries and anxieties for the future." Worrying burns the mind and consumes vital energy. If the mind is free from worries and anxieties then it is calmer and more focused and less divided to act in the present. Renounce worries, fear, and anxiety about future or outcomes by having faith in the Supreme.

After the first rung, these tendencies become 60 percent (about halfway up), then Sri Krishn says to do Karm Yog. Purify the mind, desires, Vasanas, and ego through compassionate service to others.

Then at 40 percent do spiritual practices, to bring back the wandering mind again and again. I think for that, Pranayama and focus on breath is good. Doing spiritual practices further purifies the mind and emotions towards pure devotion.

Then the ground is ready for the single pointed devotion towards a form of God that is most dear to your heart. It can be an Avatar, a deity, a Guru, Jesus, or someone else. When very little of the impurities and impressions remain, the mind can be purified through meditation and contemplation. The highest form of devotion is meditation on the formless, the cosmic consciousness.

There are different stages a devotee evolves through. First there is a need for a form, as the heart and mind are filled only in Him, and the devotee sees the divine in all forms and everywhere. The devotee then sees the divine as the essence behind all of creation and worships Him as the formless. At the peak of devotion, duality ends; in the trance of the dance of oneness the devotee becomes the beloved; there is only One. This is also the ultimate knowledge, as the destination is the same, the ultimate Truth of Oneness.

Devotion is unconditional love between me and the divine, and at the peak of devotion, the merging into the divine, I become unconditional love, bliss.

8

Meera – Incarnation of Devotion

Meera Bai epitomizes Bhakti (devotion). Her unwavering love for her Krishn was the most beautiful. Even Krishn would helplessly be drawn to her. Her conversations with Krishn poured out as poetry, as love songs for the divine (bhajans). For a devotee, all love songs are bhajans (devotion songs), and all bhajans are love songs. Hers are remembered even today.

Meera was born in the month of September 1498 to Rani Veer Kumari and Rana Ratan Singh in Kukri, a small town in the kingdom of Marwar of Rajasthan, India. When she was born, her face was as bright as the sun, so the family priest named her 'Mehra', or Meera, which means luminous. Her father belonged to the Rathore clan of Jodhpur. Rao Jodha, who established Jodhpur, was Meera's great grandfather. Her grandfather, Dudaji (Rao Duda), established the princely state of Medhta. Dudaji's eldest son, and Meera's uncle, Rana Veeram Dev, ruled Medhta, while her father was given charge of a few nearby villages including Kukri. Meera's mother was the daughter of Rana Sultan Singh of the princely Jhala Rajput family of Ratlam. Meera's mother, Veer Kumari, was very devotional and Meera used to watch her mother in prayer and worship. Meera's family were Vishnu worshipers. Her grandfather Dudaji constructed the Chaturbhuj Nath (a form of the deity Vishnu) temple. When Meera was around six years old her family went to visit a holy place in Gujarat and met with a saint there. He had with him a statue of Sri Krishn as Giridhari, with his left arm raised holding the Govardhan hill. When Meera Bai looked at the statue she went into a trance, as she was transported to her previous life as a Gopi. She remembered the time when she had watched Giridhari holding the mountain on His little finger. Meera believed she was the reincarnation of the Gopi Lalita. She fell in love with this statue that the saint carried and insisted she have it. The saint was rather startled and her father restrained her. At night, the saint had a dream, where Giridhari told him to give the statue to His dearest devotee, Meera. So the next day he did, realizing that Meera was very special to Krishn. This was Meera's awakening as a devotee of Sri Krishn. For Meera the statue was alive, and He spoke to her. She would also see Sri Krishn in her dreams. Her deep and transcendental devotion would sprout spontaneous poems for Giridhari; these were divine conversations with her beloved. Her singing was so impregnated with devotion that those in her presence would be infused with devotion and go into higher states of devotional union. Over the years, Meera's singing for Giridhari attracted many people to come and listen to her.

When Meera was around 7 years old her mother died due to childbirth and this was a big blow to Meera. She felt as though love had left her life. She felt alone and destitute. Meera went into a deep sadness and wouldn't eat or sleep, and cut herself off from others. Her father was very worried and was a broken man himself. After about a year and a half, her father also died in a battle. Now Meera had lost all the sources of unconditional love in her life. She felt helpless and alone in her grandfather's palace. The consoling by relatives was of no avail. She clung to the statue of Giridhari, who was her only support now; she never let go of Him and kept Him in bed with her as she slept. Her family had a young maid for Meera, Mithula, who became a close companion in whom she would confide and who consoled Meera. Her uncle, Rao Veeram Dev, and his son, Rao Jai Mal, took great care of Meera, but Meera always felt alone.

Her grandfather, Dudaji, was very loving and fond of Meera. He put extra attention on her education and learning. Meera was an intelligent girl and learned quickly. She wrote poems for her Giridhari with childlike innocence and love. She would also sing and dance to them, holding Giridhari in her hands. Meera used to love attending all the events where visiting saints would give sermons, or have Kirtans. Her single-pointed devotion and intensity grew more very quickly to a point where her mind was always occupied with devotional thoughts. She became known in and around Merta for her devotion towards Krishn.

Meera was now thirteen and quite free spirited thanks to her grandfather's love. Her aunt and uncle, Rao Veeram Dev, was a conservative man who didn't believe in the rights of women; he felt strongly that Meera should get married. She did not want to get married but was pressured to marry the Mewar kingdom's prince, Bhoj Raj, who was sixteen. Their wedding was in mid-April of 1511. He was the son of a very noble king, Rana Sangram Singh (Rana Sanga). Meera was very naive about worldly affairs, she didn't know how to handle in-laws, what was politically correct, or how to behave as a queen. She was also not afraid of what people would think and was very strong willed. This nature of Meera in a very conservative setting of a Rajput royal family in the sixteenth century was the perfect recipe for controversy. Meera was not interested in married life. For her, no one existed except Krishn. The in-laws frowned on this unconventional girl and gossiped about her. Meera's husband was a weak personality, and he didn't protect her from the family's antagonism, nor did he respect her devotion. Her father-in-law, however; did love and respect Meera and built a temple for her where she could worship her Giridhari. She spent most of her time in the temple and not at the palace with the family or nor did she behave like royal blood.

Sant Rai Das (Ravi Das) came to Chittaur and Meera Bai gravitated towards him with a great thirst to learn. Guru Rai Das had exceptional knowledge and devotion towards the Lord, which attracted Meera, and she was soaked in bliss when she was with him. Guru Rai Das initiated Meera as a disciple. It was after this that she sang, "Payoji maine naam ratan dhan payo. Vastu amolik di mere Sat Guru, kiripa kar apanayo". "Naam" is when a Guru initiates a disciple with a mantra for meditation. Her in-laws did not allow Meera to meet Sant Rai Das because he was of a lower caste, but she used to meet him secretly with the help of Mithula. Meera always questioned the traditions and customs of her time using logic and Vedic knowledge. She defied the caste system as a malpractice. According to her, Guru Raidas was a Brahmin, not a Sudra.

Meera's husband died in a war a few years after they married when Meera was only sixteen. Her in-laws pressurized Meera to commit Sati, an extinct tradition now where widows jumped into a pyre and burnt to death. This was especially prevalent after the Muslims invaded Bharat. When a Hindu army lost a war, before the opposing army's men could come and rape the women or take them as hostage slaves, the women would rather kill themselves through Sati. Meera refused to commit Sati, which aggravated her in-laws and royal pundits, but she was adamant that it was immoral to commit suicide, and after all, her eternal companion was Sri Krishn. After Meera's husband died, she had one saving grace, her father-in-law. He was a principled man and loved Meera, and protected her from the other family members' attacks. However; even that shelter didn't last long. She was around nineteen when her father-in-law also died. Meera's mother-in-law, sister-in-law, Uda, and brother-in-law, Vikramaditya, now king, were very cruel to Meera and tried to kill her. They wanted her to maintain the dignity of the family and act like a princess, not have a daily communion with ordinary people to sing bhajans, nor behave like a commoner. What angered them is that Meera was a rebel and an unconventional woman; she would speak back with what she thought was right or wrong. She refused to wear the veil over her head because she believed that was a custom introduced by the Muslims. This enraged her in-laws when she didn't wear it in front of them and took it as a sign of disrespect. Her in-laws wanted to control her, and have her obey their demands and expectations, and confine her to the contemporary orthodox, narrow-minded society. But she didn't fit the role of a typical woman, let alone that of a princess. She didn't care how she dressed or looked. She always wore white, being a widow. She had very little interest in home affairs, or in worldly matters, because she had completely turned inwards. She never let go of her devotion for Krishn, no matter how much anyone threatened her.

In the bleakest time of her life, when her in-laws rebuked her, and her own family didn't want her back, she sang the bhajan, "Mere to Giridhar Gopal dusaro na koi"—only Giridhar Gopal is truly my own and no other. I am wedded to that consciousness. The local society also did not approve of her unconventional ways, strong character and liberal views. She felt isolated, rejected, separated from everyone, and unloved...truly unloved. She was deeply pained and felt alone. This pain of abandonment made her devotion even more intense and single-pointed. She turned inwards more and more, immersed herself in devotion, and clung to her Giridhari - the only one who loved her unconditionally. "Teri mein to prem diwani, mero dard na jane koi" – I'm your mad lover, whose pain no one understands. Her only friend was Mithula, who was such a saving grace in her life. Mithula was also her scribe, as Meera used to go into a trance while singing for her Giridhari; Mithula used to write down the lyrics.

I don't know why her life was full of so much misery. She contemplated suicide, she had nowhere to go and leaving the in-laws was unthinkable. She was perplexed and wrote a letter to Sant Goswami Tulsidas, the leading authority of Vedic Dharma at the time, describing her situation and asking him for his advice. He wrote back to Meera saying that those who do not love the Lord should be abandoned like a thousand enemies. Abuse should never be tolerated. Finally, when she was about twenty-one, she decided to leave her in-laws. One night, she left the fort of Chittaur with deep pain in her heart, mourning, "Why don't they understand that I love Him so much!"

First, she went to Merta, where her uncle Rana Veeram Dev and cousin brother, Kuvar Rao Jai Mal, were ruling. Even though they welcomed her and took care of her, being orthodox themselves, they were not too comfortable with her leaving her in-laws and bringing shame to their family. Meera lived in Merta for a year, well taken care of. Though feeling mostly at home, she also felt rejected and betrayed by her family and missed having the unconditional love and acceptance of her late parents. She still could not fully and freely lead the spiritual life she wanted in the bounds of her family and was anxious to go to holy places, meet Gurus and saints and learn from them. She left Merta with Mithula and a band of travelers and for many days she traveled through the desert hungry and thirsty till she reached Vrindavan, the village where Sri Krishn spent his childhood with the Gopis. When she entered the Banke Bihari temple she erupted into singing, "Mharo Pranam Banke Bihari-ji," and went into a trance looking at the idol. She spent some time in the birth town of Krishn, Mathura, and Vrindavan. As she had grown older her devotion had also matured from the innocence of childhood, to the adolescent worship of her idol Krishn, to a deeper understanding of who Sri Krishn was and the knowledge He gave. She wanted to find a Guru and gain knowledge. She heard about the Goswamis of Vrindavan who were disciples of the contemporary Saint Chaitanya Mahaprabhu. They were Krishn devotees as well as scholars of Vedic knowledge. She went to meet Jiv Goswami one evening, but he refused to talk to her, saying that she was a woman and not entitled to

Vedic knowledge. Meera walked away singing, "I thought the only male (Purusha) is Krishn, the rest all female (Prakriti)," meaning there is only one consciousness, Krishn, and the rest is all creation. Struck by the deep knowledge in her words, Jiv Goswami retracted and called her back. This was followed by several sessions on Advaita Vedanta, and topics of deeper spiritual knowledge, between them. With her center in Vrindavan, she went to several pilgrimage places, including the ancient holy city of Kashi (Varanasi) where she met several saints including Sant Kabir, Sant Tulsidas, and Chaitanya Mahaprabhu. She spent time with Sant Tulsidas, hearing him sing great devotional poetry he wrote for Sri Ram, and drawn into it, she would also start singing with him. She was mesmerized by his devotion for Sri Ram and fascinated by his knowledge. It is then that Sri Ram also entered her heart.

Meera Bai came during a time when the world was showered by devotional saints. I believe Meera also traveled to Punjab and met Guru Nanak Devji. Sant Vallabhacharya, Sant Surdas, and many other saints were contemporaries of Meera.

Meera grew tired of the hypocrisy in Vrindavan and the treatment by the Pandas (temple priests) who were also jealous of her growing popularity. When she was around thirty, she left with Mithula for Dwarka in Gujarat, which had been the capital city of Sri Krishn's kingdom. Very little has been known or written about the years that Meera spent here in peace and happiness. Most people only know about her torturous years in Chittaur. In Mathura she gained great spiritual heights. She spent a lot of time in knowledge and meditation. She read the Vedanta of Sant Vallabhacharya whose works were popular at that time in Dwarka. She spent hours in meditation and higher states of consciousness. She attained divine union with her Giridhari.

"Sanson ki maala pe simron mein pee ka naam. Prem ke rang mein aisee doobi, bun gaya aik hee roop. Prem ki mala japte japte aap bani mein Shyam".

On the garland of breaths, I recite my beloved's name. Immersed so deeply into the essence of divine love, I've become one with my beloved. Chanting on the beads of devotion I've become You, my beloved Shyam.

The locals hosted her well and she rose to fame. Many years later, her youngest brother-in-law, Udai Singh, had built a new capital for Mewar, called Udaipur, with beautiful palaces. By now Meera was known throughout Bharat, and he too heard great praises of her devotion and her songs had become so famous, and were heard all over. Udai wanted Meera to come back to Mewar, her in-laws' home. Udai felt that great misfortune had fallen upon their family and kingdom after Meera left Chittor, so he sent a few people to Dwarka to convince her. She was happy in Dwarka and didn't want to go back. The priests said that they would fast unto death until she agreed to come back with them to Chittor. Perplexed, Meera didn't know what to do. One night she entered the Dwarka Dheesh temple, and in her supreme glory, her single-pointed devotion and intense longing to unite with Him, she did. At that moment she ascended into a being of divine light. When the priests went in to look for her, all they found was her white Sari (garment). She left when she was around fifty.

9

Conclusion – from the head to the heart

> *"Om Mani Padme Hum"*
> "The jewel of the mind has reached the heart's lotus."

Why is unconditional love and devotion prescribed for the present age? With so much imperfection all around that can bring anger and hatred, only love can accept and then only through love can we change and transform. Anger and hatred towards imperfection are still anger and hatred! The mind, intellect, and ego divides people. The heart, service, forgiveness, and love unites.

God distributed intellect differently and love equally. Each one has a capacity of infinite love with or without intellect.

Through devotion, our mind learns to subordinate itself to the object of devotion. In worldly life, our ego does not want to submit to anyone. Rather, it wants to take the driver's seat. It wants to dominate, manipulate and exploit others. On the other hand, in devotion our ego learns to humble itself; by taking the back seat and submitting to God, it learns to keep its likes (*raga*) and dislikes (*dvesha*) aside and fills the mind with holy thoughts.

That's why devotion is so essential in the spiritual path because in faith and devotion one has to bow one's head. Divine Grace plays a big role. The more grateful we are, more the divine light of Grace is bestowed on us!

Yoga, which is imperfect, leads you astray, off the path, stunted and malformed or stuck in *Siddhis* (spiritual powers), because Raj Yoga needs discipline, perfection in each of the eight steps, and detachment.

Spiritual knowledge (*Jnan*) that's still incomplete leads to concepts, misunderstanding, arrogance and delusion, because knowledge needs to be complete.

Devotion (*Bhakti*) though, which will remain incomplete till its culmination, will always be correct and never go wrong in any way. Each of the flavors is celebrated, whichever unique expression (*Bhaav*) is natural to you. Some feel that God is their best friend, some as their beloved, some treat the Lord like a child, some like their Master to be served, some sing the praise of the Lord, and some feel the Lord deep within as their own soul and unite with Him. All these celebrate devotion.

Bhakti bhaav (devotion ecstasy) finally merges into the divine, and the goal is reached.

There are so many reasons to celebrate devotion. Life is a journey from the head to the heart. Devotion is the one ingredient in the spiritual journey that takes you there. How?

* Devotion purifies emotions like lust, greed, and jealousy. When we turn our love towards God, when we offer ourselves to Him, the love turns to the highest; it changes from lust to love. Love for humans is selfish; it's like an insatiable thirst, which leaves us empty and deluded. But even a drop of devotion brings complete fulfillment, expansion, liberation, and bliss.
* When the heart is full of love there is compassion for everyone. It brings forth the attitude to help and serve others. If my heart is filled with devotion all the time, not only will I have sweetness and love for all, but my heart and mind will forever be pure and full of bliss.
* Mind divides, love unites. With intellect, people argue and talk about their knowledge, beliefs and opinions. We tend to disagree and debate. In devotion, there is joy in sharing songs, stories and praise for the Lord.

* The mind can get more rigid about what's right and wrong. The desire for perfection that can cause anger towards others' wrongs. Devotion takes you away from the mind to the heart where there is no right or wrong. It accepts all unconditionally. In love there is no ego; in fact, the easiest way to melt the ego is through devotion. When the sweetness of devotion fills the heart there is no anger or hatred.

* In devotion there is the nectar (*Rass*) of sweetness, joy, bliss, ecstasy, intoxication. Knowledge and Yoga are dry and incomplete without devotion.

Devotion purifies emotions. Through my personal experience, I have felt that the love that I seek is within. The love for another human always remains incomplete and imperfect. I have felt that the same love when I turned it towards God purified my emotions and thoughts; there was liberation, an expansion. I found what I was looking for that I was falsely seeking in a human.

"The essence of *Dharma* is love. Where there is no love *Dharma* cannot prosper. Dharma does not give rise to anger, jealousy, greed or passion. Dharma doesn't divide. Dharma brings people together. The best thing which brings us together is love. Love not only brings human beings together but also other live forms. Every being understands the language of love. Dogs and cats will not understand the secrets of the Upanishads but they will understand the language of love. Even ants and trees understand the language of love. Love is the essence of Dharma. Pujya Swami Chinmayananda used to say, 'Love, if not expressed makes no sense'. We should express our love. We should express our love not by giving Archie greeting cards but we should express our love through *Seva* (service). *Seva* is the expression of love. When I say I love my mother, it should be expressed through *Seva*. I cannot say I love but I will not do Seva." – Swami Nikhilananda, Chinmaya Mission.

Love is ingrained in every human being. It's our natural ability; it's our nature to love. We have been created with love. However; like anything else, love can be channeled in a positive way or a negative way. Often we see love manifesting as vices, jealousy, hatred, anger, greed, lust, and fear. Even the cruelest-hearted man loves something so much that he uses the wrong means to attain it. It is easy to flow into the gullies of negative forms of love, like anger. Then our emotions turn wild and animalistic. We lose control of the way we feel and without realizing or being aware, we become slaves to lust, greed, anger, hatred, grief, and fear. Somewhere the beauty of love is hidden in the heart of this wild beast of emotions. It needs to be churned, like butter. The butter is there everywhere in milk, but only through the process of churning does it emerge.

No, no, don't shun those negative emotions, or try so hard to get rid of them, put a lid on them, or feel guilty about them. It is better to light a candle than to curse the darkness. The wisdom of Yoga tells us to enlighten with the opposite emotion, the positive side of love and see the flowers blossom.

The seeds of love are there, planted in our hearts. Water them, then the weeds and thorns of negative emotions will automatically die.

> For lust...grow the love for the divine, experience the bliss within.
> For anger...grow the love for others, forgiveness, mercy, friendship, peace, patience, non-violence.
> For pride...grow into humility.
> For greed...grow honesty, disinterestedness, generosity, contentment, non-covetousness.
> For jealousy...grow nobility, magnanimity, complacency.
> For delusion...grow wisdom.
> For vanity, hypocrisy...grow simplicity.
> For arrogance...grow modesty.
> For cunningness and crookedness...grow straightforwardness.
> For harshness...grow mildness.
> For attachment...grow dispassion.
> For lack of faith...grow faith.
> For fickleness...grow determination.

Where there is a wild forest in the heart strewn with thorns of hatred, jealousy and many other vices, the love has turned dark with their venom. There is heartache and misery. Yet the wild, uncontrollable instincts keep fueling the fire of these demonic emotions. Wisdom is overpowered till the suffering from these vices awakens it.

Behold the love and devotion within! It is already there. Feed it with the water of awareness and the sunlight of practice and these virtues will grow a beautiful garden of love in the heart. Make preparations in your heart to receive your beloved, the Lord Himself, clean up the place and make a temple in your heart with a shrine for the divine. See the radiance of devotion emanate from within and fill your whole being, every cell. The divine is within. Now the wild beast has transformed into a divine angel. This bliss of devotion is eternal, just light a candle in the cave of your heart and see.

> *"You may turn your bones to fuel, your flesh to meat, letting them roast and sizzle in the gold-red blaze of severe austerities. But unless your heart melts in love's sweet ecstasy, you never can possess my Lord Siva, my treasure-trove."*

> *-- Tirumantiram Verse 272*

Om Tat Sat

Dedication

To Meena Om

ॐ नमो मनु मानावे प्रणाम!
सत्य कर्म प्रेम स्थापितायाः |
कृष्ण चेतना प्रकाश रुपयाः
अवतारा वरिष्ठायाः नमो नमः ॥

Om namō manu *mānāvē praṇāma!*
Satya karma prēma sthāpitāyāḥ |
Kṛṣṇa cētanā prakāśa rupayāḥ
Avatārā variṣṭhāyāḥ namō namaḥ.

Translation by Meena Om:

Manu, the first true human. Whosoever starts a new beginning, points towards a new dawn. Pranam (oblations) to that real and true human. So this *mantra* is for all sublime humans to be a superb human.

About the Author

V inita was born in Kanpur, India. She has traveled to and lived in several countries around the world. Her family lived in Zambia (Africa) for many years. She went to boarding school at St. Mary's, Nainital, India, and then college in the US.

Vinita has been a devotee of Sri Krishn and deeply spiritual from a young age, with an urge to know the Truth. After a mystical spiritual experience when she was 13, she started meditating, reading the writings of spiritual masters, and ancient texts from several faiths.

Vinita did her degree Computer Science in the US and has worked in the IT industry for more than 20 years, including management positions in leading companies such as SAP America. She currently works in IT for a company in the San Francisco bay area.

Vinita is a published author, her first book was "Eternal Way to Bliss", by John Hunt Publishing, UK. She's working on her second book, "Unfolding into Unconditional Love, and Devotion Divine".

Vinita specializes in chanting, specifically Mantras. She received her sound healing certification with internationally acclaimed teacher Jonathan Goldman. She specializes in Mantra chanting. She has done a course by Thomas Ashley-Farrand, and has a lifetime of chanting practice.

She leads meditation intensives in which she combines yoga, pranayama, meditation, healing, followed by spiritual knowledge discussions.

She has been a teacher with the Art of Living Foundation, taken several courses and practiced for many years.

She has also given several talks and led workshops at public events, organizations, community centers, libraries, colleges, and companies for over 15 years. Vinita is enthusiastic about volunteering and has been involved in several service projects for non-profit organizations.

Under the tutelage of the Chinmaya Mission she has studied the following texts:

Tattva Bodha. Atma Bodha. Narad Bhakti Sutra. Patanjali Yoga Sutras. Isha Upanishad. Kena Upanishad. Katho Upanishad. Chhandogya Upanishad. Kaivalya Upanishad. Bhagavad Gita. Ashtavakra Gita. Yoga Vasistha. Kapila Gita. Sadacarah. Aparoksanubhuti. Mahabharat. Ramayan, Srimad Bhagavatam, and other minor texts.

She has also studied the teachings of Shankaracharya, Vivekananda, Ramana Maharishi, Sri Sri Ravi Shankar, and many others.

She has been studying ancient wisdom, mystical traditions, religions, quantum physics, Ayurveda, Yoga, meditation, sound vibrations and holistic well-being for over 25 years. Her innate nature is that of devotion and mysticism.